MW01268008

devotion explosion

What to do when your quiet time
becomes too quiet

Stephen Schwambach

BROADMAN
& HOLMAN
PUBLISHERS
Nashville, Tennessee

devotion
explosion

Published by Broadman & Holman Publishers,
Nashville, Tennessee
Acquisitions & Development Editor: Janis Whipple
Interior Design: Steven Boyd
Printed in the United States of America

4260-83
0-8054-6083-7

Dewey Decimal Classification: 242
Subject Heading: DEVOTIONAL LITERATURE / BIBLE—STUDY
Library of Congress Card Catalog Number: 96-14792

Unless otherwise noted, Scripture quotations are from the
Holy Bible, New International Version, copyright © 1973,
1978, 1984 by International Bible Society.

Library of Congress Cataloging-in-Publication Data
Schwambach, Stephen
    Devotion explosion : what to do when your quiet time
becomes too quiet / Stephen Schwambach
        p.   cm.
    ISBN 0-8054-6083-7 (pb)
    1. Bible—Devotional use. 2. Bible—Study and teaching.
3. Bible—Reading. 4. Spiritual life—Baptists. 5. Baptists—
Membership. I. Title.
BS617.8.S38 1996
248.3—dc20

96-14792
CIP

96 97 98 99 00 5 4 3 2 1

. . . .

To the congregation I pastor—
if you hadn't said a long time ago that I could
write books as part of my ministry to you,
this book could never have happened.
Thanks for loving me and letting
me be me, instead of trying to
force me to be the kind of
pastor all the other
churches have.

▼

Contents

Contents

OK, gonna go out on a limb here . . .

My guess is that your devotional life stinks.

No? OK, fine. My mistake. I should have known. Your devotional life is electrifying. You haven't missed a day of quiet time in ten years. As a result, you've reached Spiritual Level 777 and have become God's best friend—hanging out with the Big Guy right alongside Moses, David, Paul, and John.

As a matter of fact, the only reason you're holding this book in your hands at this very moment is that there's this "friend" of yours whose walk with God is truly pathetic.

This friend of yours knows he should be having daily devotions. But his dirty little secret (discovered only by you through the shrewd employment of your unusually perceptive gift of discernment) is this: He ain't doin' it. He's not even coming close.

God knows he's tried. But no matter how mercilessly he has berated himself over the depth of his spiritual depravity, he can't string together thirty straight days of quiet time to save his life.

1

He knows that the only lasting cure for his spiritual lethargy is a daily prayer encounter with God, coupled with an in-depth study of the Bible. However, because he can't make himself do this one little thing, he is absolutely eaten up with guilt.

Here's what bugs him the most. The terrible truth is that he enjoys scanning the back of a cereal box far more than he likes reading his Bible. He can talk favorite movies for a solid hour with a total stranger, but he can't keep his mind from wandering during a five-minute conversation with the Savior of his sorry soul.

You were going to buy this book for *that* poor guy, weren't you?

Bless your selfless, generous heart. To think that you would condescend to help this barely saved, despicable specimen of riffraff pewdom helps me understand why you're the spiritual giant you are.

Well, now. Don't be ashamed to march this book right to the cash register, look that clerk straight in the eye, and say, "Bag it!"

The clerk will not judge you for two reasons.

1. The only bookstores permitted to stock this book are those who train their clerks to carefully avert their eyes from the title of any book they sell, so as not to embarrass the purchaser. So far as she knows, you have handed her a book titled, *How to Stay Spiritually Superior.*

2. To protect you from those employees who peek, we have notified all bookstores that this book will be purchased solely by people who do not need it.

Feel better? Good.

Now hurry up and buy this thing.

Your friend is waiting.

1

My qualifications for writing this book

You may wonder how I know so much about people who have anemic devotional lives.

Well, I'm a pastor. I counsel the depraved. These despicable worms slink into my office and confess their filthy . . . ah, well, actually . . . no.

The real reason I know so much about these lowly vermin is that I was one of them. In fact, for the first fifteen years of my ministry, I laid guilt trip after guilt trip on the members of my congregation, urging them to practice the very thing I myself struggled to do.

Do I sound as though I was a hypocrite? I didn't mean to be.

What would happen is, I would start spending, say, two hours each day in personal devotions. I'd get a pretty good run of several weeks going—after which time I would pulpiteer on the priceless virtues of intimate connectedness to God.

Then I'd get so busy that I'd fall off the wagon for several days or a week or two. Aaaargh! I'd be so devastated by my inconsistency that I couldn't preach another word on the subject. I'd stay absolutely quiet about quiet time for six months.

Then I'd get on another daily devotional roll, thinking I'd finally found the moral character I once lacked—and the cycle would start all over again.

I have just shared my personal, private prescription for creating a magnificently dysfunctional congregation. But when I tried to patent this powerful procedure, my application was turned down.

"Sorry," they said. "Ninety-five percent of the churches in America are run this way. You'll have to come up with something a little more unique."

Bummer. I was sure I had finally found my place in leadership history, my own special area of pastoral giftedness.

Then, on one of my "good days," I stumbled across a passage of Scripture that contained a totally unique devotional technique. I'd never heard of it before. Desperate, afraid to hope, I tried it.

It worked. It worked for one month, then two. It worked that entire year, then another. That was twelve years ago. And it's still working.

I'm not going to tell you I haven't missed a day of quiet time in twelve years. My life is too complex, my responsibilities too great, my personality too warped to make that realistic. But how does 340 or 350 days out of a year sound? Except for a couple of years when I dipped down closer to 300, that's been the norm.

How do I account for the difference? I no longer do daily devotions out of a sense of dreaded duty. The technique I have discovered—and over the years tweaked to near-perfection—is so exciting, so compelling, so rewarding, that my time with God has gone from quiet to explosive.

Quite simply, my devotions have become my favorite part of any day—and that's the honest-to-goodness truth, even though I lead a fascinating, varied, highly productive (OK—occasionally productive) life. Ninety-nine days out of a hundred, I can't wait to begin my intimate time with God. Nine times out of ten, I'm genuinely sorry when I have to pull away and go on to something else.

It's changed my life. It can change yours too. This secret is transferable. Better yet, it's easy. Anybody can do it.

Are you intrigued enough to keep reading? Well, come on, then. Time's a-wastin'.

2

What if . . .

What if I could show you a new way to do your daily quiet time that would:

▼ Help you actually look forward to your devotions nine days out of ten?

▼ Enable you to get more out of reading your Bible than ever before?

▼ Keep your mind from wandering when you pray?

▼ Fit whatever time slot you have for your devotions on any given day—from five minutes to an hour or more?

▼ Perfectly suit your personality?

▼ Heighten your reverence for God?

▼ Improve your ability to memorize Scripture painlessly. Hmmm. Would you settle for, "Improve your ability to memorize Scripture with *reduced* pain"?

▼ Transform your quiet time with God into your favorite thing to do?

▼ Increase your love for Jesus?

▼ Deepen your understanding of difficult scriptural passages?

▼ Cause you to be loathe to quit when it's time to stop, at least half the time?

▼ Enhance your capacity to actually put God's Word into practice?

▼ Assure you and those who come after you of a brighter future?

▼ Draw you into an intimacy with the Holy Spirit unlike anything you have ever known?

▼ Eliminate poverty, retire the national debt, and make you a millionaire in two weeks or less? (Actually, my plan won't significantly affect poverty, the national debt, or your personal wealth. Not in two weeks, anyway. I just wanted to see if you were paying attention.)

▼ Ignite a **DEVOTION EXPLOSION!** right in the middle of your sleepy quiet time?

If I could show you such a thing, would you be interested?

Well, you're in luck.* That's exactly what I'm about to do—starting in the very next chapter.

3

First things first: You gotta have an attitude

"Martha, Martha, . . . you are worried and upset about many things, but only one thing is needed."
Luke 10:41–42

You think you're too busy for daily devotions?

You're right. You are. In fact, with all the fires you keep having to put out because you have no time to develop a relationship with the Fire Chief, I can guarantee that you will be too busy for daily devotions for the rest of your life.

You think you can keep your daily appointment with the Lord God Almighty, the Creator of the universe, and the Savior of your worthless soul

---

* Please forgive me for using the phrase, "you're in luck." I know better. I don't believe in luck. Luck is not one of your more prominent biblical teachings—though in Ecclesiastes 9:11, Solomon makes it sound as though such a thing might possibly exist. But we all know what a melancholy snit he was in when the Holy Spirit inspired him to write *that* book.

I said, "you're in luck," because it sounded a little too megalomaniac to say, "I believe the book you now hold in your hands, written by yours truly, may be, in God Almighty's exquisite, sovereign timing, your last, best hope to stop your backsliding, get off this spiritual plateau you've been stuck on forever and get your spiritual life in gear—before God has to do something really drastic to get your attention." That is closer to what I believe than, "you're in luck." But I decided it would be better if I didn't mention it.

on the same sloppy, hit-and-miss basis you've been subsisting on up to now?

You're right. You can.

And never know what might have been.

I've got an untested theory about hell. I think everybody will be given his own big-screen television, complete with Surround Sound. Furthermore, I don't think the people who go there will much notice the flames. I think the pain of the fire will pale beside the agony of what's showing on every channel of everyone's personal TV: a detailed, full-color maxi-series of everything they could have become, had they fully surrendered to Jesus.

Not you, of course. You're not going to hell if you've discovered and accepted a personal relationship with Jesus. Thank God, neither am I. But when I think of what my own maxi-series of squandered opportunities looks like, I get the shakes.

As a result, I've developed an attitude.

Correction. I've developed an Attitude.

Let me restate that. I've developed: an ATTITUDE!

Jesus first. Jesus foremost. Jesus or nothing.

If I've spent One-on-one with Him the portion of this day that I feel in my heart He wants to spend with me, I'm already a stunning success. Anybody else I talk to and any other cotton-pickin' thing I happen to accomplish for the rest of the day is nothing but the side dish. My time with Him is the main course.

However, if I move mountains today and ignore my precious Jesus, relegating Him to the back burner of "Sorry-Lord-I-got-covered-up-but-I-sure-hope-You-understand," I am a hollowed-out shell of a failure. I've lived long enough to watch every mountain I ever built at the expense of my relationship with Christ crumble to the ground, fall short of its promise, or become a mountainous curse.

They can fire me. My wife can leave me. My kids can spit on my grave. But I'm gonna do whatever it takes to be *best friends* with You, Jesus.

If there's anything that matters more to you than knowing God and experiencing Him, Satan will find it and shove it smack dab in front of your face. And right there your fat idol will stay with a cocky leer on its face, until the day you pick up the biggest sledgehammer you can find and smash it to a thousand bits.

You and God. Period.

Nothing else can take the place of the exquisitely sweet intimacy of our love life, when it's just You and me. Nothing.

▼ Not my Sunday morning corporate worship experience.

▼ Not my Sunday School class.

▼ Not my small group Bible study.

▼ Not my ministry.

▼ Not any of the work I do for You.

▼ Not any of the sacrifices I make for You.

You are All. Beside You there is no other. Everything and everybody else that tries to take Your Holy of Holies place in my life can go take a flying leap.

> *If anyone comes to me and does not hate his father and mother, his wife and children, his brothers and sisters—yes, even his own life—he cannot be my disciple.*
>
> Luke 14:26

But whatever was to my profit I now consider loss for the sake of Christ. What is more, I consider everything a loss compared to the surpassing greatness of knowing Christ Jesus my Lord, for whose sake I have lost all things. I consider them rubbish, that I may gain Christ and be found in him. . . . I want to know Christ and the power of his resurrection and the fellowship of sharing in his sufferings, becoming like him in his death, and so, somehow, to attain to the resurrection from the dead.

Philippians 3:7–11

Apart from me you can do nothing.

John 15:5b

That's the Attitude.

DEVOTION EXPLOSION! will help you get that Attitude and keep it.

But you're going to have to go directly to the Holy Spirit who dwells in you and get some of it from Him right now, or you'll never even try **DEVOTION EXPLOSION!**

Without at least a mustard seed's worth of that Attitude to get you launched, you may as well throw this book in the trash for all the good it's going to do you.

4

This is it!

I'm about to show you how to experience your own personal **DEVOTION EXPLOSION!**

. . . .

First: Do you think you can manage to read through each of these steps with an open mind? If you're unsure, ask God right now to help you do it this once. It'll make things a whole lot easier on both of us if you can.

I promise you that each technique is straight out of the Bible. In the chapters that follow, I'll share with you the scriptural source for each, along with my secrets for tailor-making them to perfectly fit your personality.

If you think you may have tried something similar before, please try to suspend your skepticism until you've heard me completely. Chances are, this system is different from anything you've done in the past. Trust me.

And keep in mind, this is a package. The whole is greater than the sum of its parts. Before you blow it off, I'm going to challenge you to try the whole enchilada for one month.

If at the end of that time you absolutely despise my system, you can write me a nasty note. Here— I'll even give you my home address so you can make sure it reaches me personally:

Stephen Schwambach
The White House
1600 Pennsylvania Avenue NW
Washington, D.C. 20500

See? I told you that you could trust me.

So, are you ready? Take a deep breath and let's go.

For the next thirty days, here's what you're gonna do:

1. Pick a book of the Bible and write it out, word-for-word.

. . . .

2. Turn to your computer or typewriter and type out your prayer. When you're finished, delete it.

3. Note the verses that leap out at you and memorize them—but only when you're in the mood.

You probably can't wait to hear my scriptural basis for memorizing Bible verses only when you're in the mood, can you? Or how about my verse for computer prayer? Hey—I've got 'em! One of our staff members at the church I pastor says that when it suits my purposes, I can proof-text with the best of them.

▼

PART 1

Your
One-of-a-Kind
Bible

Here's how to create your own ***DEVOTION EXPLOSION!***
Scripture pages, step by step.

1. Select a book of the Bible assigned to you by the
Holy Spirit.

2. Ask God to open your heart, soul, mind, spirit,
and will to the Word you are about to write.

3. Ask the Holy Spirit to speak to you as you write.

4. Read aloud a short phrase, savoring it, and
absorbing its meaning.

5. Write out the phrase on one of the ***DEVOTION
EXPLOSION!*** pages we have provided (see pp.103–106).

6. Continue as long as you like, phrase by phrase,
verse by verse.

7. Put an asterisk beside any word or phrase that
sheds important light on some other Scripture passage you know.

. . . .

8. Write the book, chapter, and verse of that other passage in the provided margin, creating a cross-reference for better understanding.

9. Record in your **DEVOTION EXPLOSION!** notebook (see chap. 13) anything that makes you go, "Hmmm!" "Huh-oh!" or "Wow!" Include the date, time, and Scripture reference, along with the message you believe God may be giving you.

10. In the slot marked "Study," jot down the reference of any passage you would like to study later.

11. In the slot marked "Memorize," jot down the reference of any passage you would like to hide in your heart through memorization.

12. When you reach a stopping place or you're out of time, thank the Lord for the unspeakable privilege of so intimately handling His Word.

13. Keep your **DEVOTION EXPLOSION!** Scripture pages with you the rest of the day.

14. Pick up tomorrow where you left off today.

▼

5

You've gotta be kidding—write out my own Bible?

No, you don't have to write out the entire Bible. But I do believe you ought to own at least one book of the Bible in your own handwriting. Why? Take a look at Deuteronomy 17:18–20:

> When he [the king] takes the throne of his kingdom, he is to write for himself on a scroll a copy of this law, taken from that of the priests, who are Levites. It is to be with him, and he is to read it all the days of his life so that he may learn to revere the LORD his God and follow carefully all the words of this law and these decrees and not consider himself better than his brothers and turn from the law to the right or to the left. Then he and his descendants will reign a long time over his kingdom in Israel.

Perhaps the same question occurs to you that occurred to me the first time I really paid attention to that passage: "Now, why would God command every king of Israel to write out for himself a copy of the Bible, to keep it with him, and to read it all the days of his life? Kings are busy! Sounds like a job that ought to be delegated, like we do to Bible publishers today. Were there no scribes available?"

And then I asked another question: "Could it be that there's something about what happens when you write out sacred Scripture that you can experience no other way?"

And another: "Could it be that we human beings are far more likely to grasp, agree with, and internalize the Word of God when we read it in our own handwriting?"

Then I looked at the five promises God made to the king who dared to obey His command to write out the Word:

1. He would learn to revere the Lord.

2. He would learn to follow carefully all the words he had written.

3. He would learn not to consider himself better than his brothers.

4. He would not turn from God's Word.

5. As a result, he and his descendants would reign a long time.

I wanted all five of those wonderful promises to come true in my life. But would they also apply to me? After all, I wasn't a king. Or was I? What about 1 Peter 2:9? Doesn't that passage identify Christians as a "royal" priesthood? And what about 2 Timothy 2:12? Doesn't it say we will "reign" with Christ?

A prickling sensation began to make its way up my spine. As I read the passage over and over, talked it through with a handful of deeply spiritual friends, and prayed about it, I became convinced that these promises were applicable to all of God's people. Scripturally, I could find no reason why their substantial blessings could not be legitimately appropriated by anyone who met the conditions.

Then came the questions. Tough ones. Was I willing to meet those rather unusual conditions? Did I want to actually haul out a piece of paper and write down the Word, verse by verse, chapter by chapter? How much would I have to write before these stunning promises began to take effect? A page? A whole book of the Bible?

I had never met anyone who had written out the Bible. In fact, I had never even heard of anyone now living who had done so.

For me, it was decision time. Just as it soon will be for you.

6

Has anybody else tried this radical plan?

In 1983, I took the plunge. Using some leftover blank paper from a loose-leaf Bible, I chose to write out the Book of Proverbs, which had always been one of my favorites.

That very first day, I began to discover why God had commanded His kings to write out their own, personal copies of the Scriptures.

As the Word of God began to flow from my eyes, through my brain, down my arm, into my pen, and onto paper, I thought, *This must be something like what the prophets felt, as they penned Your sacred Scriptures for the very first time.* I got goose bumps, just thinking about it.

What's more, the entire process slowed me down to a richly absorptive pace that enabled me to *at least* double my understanding of God's Word. Why? Well, think about it. First, I would read the phrase I was about to copy. Then I would automatically read it again as I copied it, often glancing back and forth, to make sure I had it letter-perfect.

The act of retaining each phrase in my mind long enough to accurately write it grooved my brain differently and more deeply than if I had merely allowed my eyes to fly across the page. Plus, there was the physical motion that goes along with writing anything out by hand. I was literally forming the Word of God, stroke by stroke, letter by letter, word by word, phrase by phrase, verse by verse.

Unlike what all too often happened when I merely read my Bible, my mind didn't wander, forcing me to reread the passage two or three times, just to make some sense of it. The very act of recording God's own words focused me on its meaning as never before.

Early on, I found it helped to read each phrase aloud as I wrote it. Without realizing it at first, I was bringing the power of another promise into this gripping experience. In Romans 10:17, God says that "faith comes from *hearing* the message" (emphasis mine). I was actually increasing my faith with each word of God that I spoke, heard, and wrote.

Wow. Talk about a total sensory experience. I was *seeing* the Word. I was *hearing* the Word. I was *feeling* the Word as it flowed through my fingertips onto paper. I was even *tasting* the Word as I spoke it, for the first time identifying with the exuberance of the writer in Psalm 119:103: "How sweet are your words to my taste, sweeter than honey to my mouth!"

Lest you think the only one of the five senses untouched was my sense of smell, think again. As my understanding of Christ through His Word increased by leaps and bounds, my nostrils were filled with "the fragrance of the knowledge of him" (2 Cor. 2:14).

I was totally unprepared for the magnitude of its impact. In all my years of Bible reading, Bible listening, Bible study, and Bible preaching, nothing I had ever experienced touched this. Nothing else even came close. I was in awe.

Talk about a buzz, a natural high. This was better by far. This was a *supernatural* high. I felt connected to Almighty God in a way that I had never known before.

The level of intimacy and closeness I shared with Him as I wrote was inexplicable, at first. Why all of this from merely writing some words on paper? Sure, it was the Bible and all, but—and then it hit me. "In the beginning was the Word, and the Word was with God, and the Word was God (John 1:1). God doesn't just speak words. He *is* the Word.

Stumbling along, I had somehow approached this entire process out of the obedience that comes from blind faith. Having read Deuteronomy 17:18–20, I had not brushed it off as an historical oddity. Instead, the Spirit had quickened it to my heart and enabled me to believe that what I had read was not only true, but that it was fully applicable to my life.

And that changed everything. Suddenly, I wasn't merely writing words. I was writing *The Word*.

Because of God's inexplicable, undeserved gift of faith, it wasn't words that were flowing through me as I wrote. It was *The Word*, God Himself. No wonder this wasn't "devotions as usual." No wonder this far surpassed any "quiet time" I had ever known.

I had just experienced my first **DEVOTION EXPLOSION!**

And I became addicted. I know that's probably not the most spiritual word I could have chosen, but if addicted means "can't wait to do it again," then that's what I was.

I finished the Book of Proverbs, but I wasn't nearly ready to quit. I figured I'd balance things out with something short from the New Testament, so after chatting with the Lord about it, I wrote out the Book of James.

But that went by way too fast. If anything, I was even more eager to write out the Word now than when I had first begun. This was exactly the opposite of every other devotional system I had ever tried. My old pattern had been to work myself into an emotional frenzy the first week, only to run out of steam before the month was out.

But I discovered that writing out the Word wasn't built on emotion. This was built on the rock-solid foundation of God's Word, by faith. And His power in my life was growing.

After another chat with the Lord, I decided to tackle the longest book of the Bible: Psalms. *This will keep me busy for a while,* I thought. And it did. But when I wrote the last word of the 150th chapter, I was completely, irrevocably hooked.

"What's going on here, Lord?" I asked. And then, the question that had been building within me for some time: "Do You want me to write out the whole thing?"

The very idea terrified me. We were talking years here. What if I started to write out the entire Bible, only to falter midway and fail to reach my goal? Still, I couldn't deny the life-changing impact it was having on me.

I decided to take it a book a time, alternating the Old Testament with the New. Even if I got tired and quit along the way, I reasoned, I would accomplish light years more than I had dared dream at the start.

First came Matthew. Then Genesis. Then Mark. Then Exodus. I admit that the genealogies were somewhat less exciting than the Beatitudes, but this is the absolute truth: Even during those periods when I spent day after day doing nothing but writing out verses like, "from the tribe of Benjamin, Palti son of Raphu," I didn't come close to quitting. That's the amazing thing. I kept right on going. That kind of consistency wasn't like me at all.

And so it was, that on my son Abraham's eighth birthday—Thursday, June 1st, 1995, at 6:10 A.M., I stretched out full-length on the floor, face down, and wept my gratitude to God. Moments before, I had just written the last word of the last verse of the Book of Malachi, completing a twelve-year journey of two testaments, 66 books, 1,189 chapters, 31,173 verses and 807,361 words.

The entire Bible. In my own handwriting. Unbelievable.

So, what am I saying? That you should go and do likewise? Not at all. In fact, the very idea is so daunting that I want you to put the idea of writing the entire Bible totally out of your mind.

Instead, let me repeat what I said in the last chapter: Every Christian should own at least one book of the Bible in his or her own handwriting. Just one book. That's all. That much you can do.

Which one? Why not ask the Lord? Since, by the time you finish writing this one book, you will know it, understand it, and love it like no other book of the Bible, shouldn't it be the one you most want to impact your life? Shouldn't it be the one you most need?

Only the Lord, in His intimate wisdom and knowledge of you as your Creator, knows which of His books will do that for you. So ask Him. He'll tell you.

Oh. One more thing. If you think His answer is the Book of Jude, I'd recommend that you go back and check with Him one more time.

7

What goes where?

You are about to create a book of the Bible that is totally unique. It will be as individualized as your signature, as personal as your fingerprint.

For an explanation of how to create and use your enclosed *DEVOTION EXPLOSION!* pages, please take a look at the sample on the opposite page.

1. The book of the Bible you are writing goes here.

. . . .

2. If this is the left page, the chapter in which you are writing at the top of the page goes here. If this is the right page, the chapter in which you are writing at the bottom of the page goes here.

The Devotion Explosion! Scripture Pages

Book _____**1**_____ Chapter __**2**__ Verse __**3**__ Date __**4**__

Scripture	Notes
5	**6**

Study:_____**7**_____ Memorize:_____**8**_____

□ Quoted Scripture list □ Memorized new Scripture □ Wrote in commentary □ Prayed
9   **10**   **11**   **12**

Page
13

. . . .

3. If this is the left page, the first full verse you are writing at the top of the page goes here. If this is the right page, the last verse on the page (even if you don't have room for the whole verse) goes here.

4. Put the date you began writing this page here.

5. It is in this column that you will actually write out the Word of God.

6. This column gives you room to make brief notes or include other Scripture references beside the passage you are writing out.

7. Write in here any subject or Scripture reference that you would like to study in-depth at a later time.

8. Did you find a passage you would love to commit to memory? Write the reference here.

9. Check this box if you quoted your list of memory Scriptures today.

10. Check this box if you started memorizing a new verse today or if you spent a little time working on a verse that you haven't yet perfectly memorized.

11. Did the Holy Spirit impress you strongly enough on a topic as you were writing out the Word that you made some notes in your **DEVOTION EXPLOSION!** notebook? If so, check this box.

12. Check here if you met your prayer goal for today.

13. Insert a running page count here, going back to the beginning of the book of the Bible you are writing.

14. This one is the most important of all. (Just kidding. There is no #14.)

8

Do I hafta say it out loud?

Do you have to say the Word out loud as you write it? No. But when you get finished reading this chapter, you'll want to. Why? Because it will increase your faith. Romans 10:17 says that faith comes by "hearing" the Word of God.

That's a pretty famous verse. If you've been going to a Bible-preaching church for any length of time, I'll bet you've heard it more than once. Verse eight of that same chapter, however, is one we often overlook: "The word is near you; it is in *your mouth* and in your heart" (emphasis mine).

I don't fully understand why, but I can testify that it's true: There is a direct connection between having God's Word in *your* mouth and depositing it deeply into your heart. The effect is that you sense God's comforting, empowering Word very, very near.

Sure, it can be motivating to hear your pastor preach the Word. It's great to have Scripture tapes going like crazy during your commute to work. But there is nothing quite like hearing your own squeaky voice speak the very words of God to cause you to internalize and personalize the intimacy of His message.

When you hear yourself speak the Word, you own it.

"But what if somebody overhears me talking to myself? Won't he think I'm nuts?"

Probably. But it's been way too long since you've been persecuted for Jesus. Wear it like a badge.

"What will my family members think?"

I don't know what yours will think, but let me conclude this chapter by telling you about one of mine. I began writing out the Word in 1983—the same year we adopted our daughter Abigail, bringing her into our home when she was five days old.

There's no other way to put it: in her little-girl years, Abi was, and is, a daddy's girl. While the others read, watched television, or played, Abi chose to be near me. Naturally, I ate it up.

While my favorite time for devotions is early in the morning, for the first five years of her life, I also wrote out the Word just before bed. Sometimes that ended up being pretty late.

Night after night, Abi would go to her room for her sleeping bag and pillow, drag them into the kitchen, and make a pallet on the floor beside the kitchen table while I wrote out the Word. Invariably, she would fall asleep as she listened to me saying the Word out loud.

One night I got in unusually late. I was dog tired. I mean stumbling, falling-down tired. Abi had held out waiting for me as long as she could, but when I shuffled into the kitchen to find her, there she was on the floor, fast asleep.

I decided I just didn't have it in me to do devotions that night. "I'll double up tomorrow night," I told myself. So I carefully scooped her up and deposited her in her bed.

Along about 2:00 A.M., I was sawing logs when I gradually became aware of a presence. It was Abi, standing beside my bed in her pajamas.

"Daddy?" she whispered in a teary voice, "Aren't you going to write out the Word?"

Only she didn't say it like that. What she really said, in her four-year-old voice, was, "Daddy? Ahun't you gonna wite out the Wood?"

Good grief.

I lay there for a long moment, listening to her sniffle, as she tried to fight back her little-girl tears. Talk about guilt trips. I heaved a great sigh and threw back the covers.

"Where are you going?" my sleepy wife mumbled.

"Where else?" I replied. "Ah'm gonna go wite out the Wood."

9

Hmmm! . . . Huh-oh! . . . Wow!

There is one really bothersome hassle that keeps coming up during a typical *DEVOTION EXPLOSION!* Frankly, I've been hiding it from you, because I wanted you to think this whole thing is a breeze.

But last night I had trouble sleeping. The guilt of my cover-up finally got to me so bad that I decided to come clean.

Until now, I've tried to make you think that all you have to do is sit yourself down, write out the Word, jot a little note here and there, and, slick as olive oil on a brass doorknob, you're ready for a high-tech prayer trek on your trusty computer. Well, not really.

Remember when I waxed eloquent about how your understanding of the Word of God would at least double as you wrote out the Word? Yeah, well, I told the truth. And truth to tell, it's a real bother.

You'll be zipping along, writing out Scripture, minding your own business, everything going as smoothly as I promised—when all at once—*Boom!* Seemingly out of nowhere, a stunningly powerful insight from God's Word will explode inside your head.

You'll shake your noggin to clear your mind, trying to keep on writing so you can stay on the ambitious schedule you've set for yourself. Fat chance. Your brain will be in a state of shock from the revelation the Holy Spirit just dropped on you. Try as you might, you won't be able to make it go away.

When this happens—and bless God anyhow, it does all the time while you're innocently trying to write out the Word—you'll begin to appreciate why I was forced to call this thing *DEVOTION EXPLOSION!* Now you know.

Look, please don't get mad at me and return the book, OK? Tell you what. To make up for my deception, I'll let you in on the secret of what to do when one of these interruptive explosions occurs—how's that? Would you agree to keep the book then? Would 'ja, huh, would 'ja?

My dozen years of experience with these little explosions is that they come in three major varieties. I've devoted a short, punchy little chapter to each.

10

Explosions that make you go, "Hmmm!"

These are the puzzlers, the biblical truths that don't at all fit your preconceptions of the way God acts, the world works, or Christians are supposed to behave. This is the stuff you always used to overlook when you were reading twenty chapters a day, trying to play catch-up in the month of December on your "Through the Bible in a Year" plan.

For instance, did you ever run across that little sleeper in 1 Kings 22? I'd read it before. Had to have. But it wasn't until I was writing the thing out for myself that my eyes got big and I started doing some serious wondering about what was going on.

According to Micaiah the prophet, the Lord was sitting on His throne, a buncha angels hanging out on His right and left. All at once, the Lord initiates this brainstorming session. He asks the group: "Who will entice Ahab into attacking Ramoth Gilead and going to his death there?" (1 Kings 22:20).

Yeah, well, different angels pose various solutions, but none of them really catches God's attention. Finally, a spirit steps forward and says he's got an idea. God's all ears. This nice, kind, heavenly being says: "I will go out and be a lying spirit in the mouths of all his prophets" (1 Kings 22:22).

God likes the plan and says beautiful, that'll work. You've got the job. Go for it.

So help me—according to Micaiah, that's exactly what happened. As a matter of fact, he goes on to say that it was the Lord who put a lying spirit in the mouths of Ahab's prophets.

Of course, in a show of appreciation for this little tidbit of behind-the-scenes insight, good ol' Zedekiah (one of those prophets in whose mouth that lying spirit had been just a-yammering away) walked up to Micaiah and slapped him right in the face.

Well, you coulda slapped me in the face too. It wouldn't have stunned me any more than the Holy Spirit did when I wrote out this eye-popping chapter.

As a matter of fact, the last thing you want to do after a head-on collision between the Word of God and your comfortable presuppositions is to try to brush it off or pretend it didn't happen. I think you'll agree: This is one of those explosions that makes you go, "Hmmmm!"

So right after you discover you've barely survived the blast, write out your concerns. Quickly list all the questions the passage raises. Then , even if you don't have time to dig into it at that precise moment, your dynamic, on-the-spot, eyewitness notes will be there waiting for you when you're ready to do some serious Bible study and sink your teeth into something truly substantial.

How and where will you write all this down? Glad you asked.

But first, let me quickly describe the other two kinds of explosions you're likely to encounter. Then I'll give you the scoop on how to deal with all three of them at once.

Fair enough?

Explosions that make you go,"Huh-oh!"

The "Huh-ohs!" are the explosions that tag you offbase. Did I say, "tag"? Actually, they blow your whole leg off.

When one of these babies goes off in the middle of your devotions, you'll discover what I did: They ain't conventional. We're talkin' nuclear. God likes to detonate one of these lethal devices just about the time you're feelin' smug and snug as a bug in a rug.

Like what happened to me when I innocently happened across 2 Corinthians 5:15: "And he died for all, that those who live should no longer live for themselves but for him who died for them and was raised again."

Peeled the skin right off me, head to toe. That verse ripped into the heart of a secret sin that has always been one of my biggest weaknesses: I can come up with more strategies to do the will of God in such a way that, lo and behold, will benefit me! That's right. Yours truly, gettin' public credit for living for God, when all the while, I'm doin' somethin' awful close to livin' for myself.

The megatonnage from that explosion was so great that I had to put it on my memorization list. I wish I could say that all that selfish, manipulative behavior is completely behind me, but that cotton-pickin' verse is still doin' a "Just As I Am" altar call number on me every time I quote it. The gray ash fallout from that explosion is still coming down.

The thing is, I know for a fact that I had read that verse twenty or thirty times before, if I had read it once. But it never detonated, penetrating my thick hide with its searing truth, until the day I read it in my own handwriting.

12

Explosions that make you go, "Wow!"

If you *have* to have something blow up in your face, I recommend this one. Thank God I get these more than any other. They're all over the place in the Word, everywhere you write.

One of my all-time favorite eruptions occurred while writing out Zechariah 3:1–7. There's old Joshua, standing before the angel of the Lord, dressed in the filthy rags of his sin, Satan just a-givin' him what-for. All of a sudden, the Lord jumps in and comes to sinful old Joshua's defense: "The LORD rebuke you, Satan! The LORD, who has chosen Jerusalem, rebuke you! Is not this man a burning stick snatched from the fire?"

If I had ever heard a description of a Bible hero I could identify with, this was it.

Tears sprang to my eyes. *That's what I am!* I thought. *I'm nothing but a burning stick, snatched from the fire. But the Lord! Bless His holy Name, the*

Lord defends stinking, blackened, smoking, burning sticks!

By the time I read on, to see that the angel of the Lord removed Joshua's sin, clothed him in righteousness, and then gave him a shot at heaven's big time, I was blown away. Even for a "decent and in order" guy like I am, it was shoutin' time.

I fell on my face to the floor and told God I wanted in on this one. That very day I started hiding those seven verses in my heart and I haven't dropped them off my essential memorization list yet. Shoot, I even preached a seven-week Wednesday night series on them, doing my best to blow apart my whole congregation as well.

See what I'm saying? Trouble. That's what these *DEVOTION EXPLOSIONS!* are, nothin' but trouble. So the question is, how do you deal with these bombs when they go off?

13

The Devotion Explosion! notebook

Are you ready for this? You need to go out and buy a special notebook. I know, I know, more expense. But this is really important. Your peace of mind is worth it. Label the thing "*DEVOTION EXPLOSIONS!*" and keep it nearby anytime you write out the Word.

Divide your notebook into three sections, one for each of the eventualities we just covered:

Section One: "Hmmm!"

Section Two: "Huh-oh!"

Section Three: "Wow!"

When you run into one of those 1 Kings 22 chapters, turn to Section One and log your entry. Obviously, a passage similar to 2 Corinthians 5:15 would go in Section Two, and a Zechariah 3:1–7 explosion would be recorded in Section Three.

List each entry with the date and Scripture reference. You might even want to get fancy and write the subject out in the margin for easy reference when you come back to your notebook later, "loaded for bare" and ready to do some serious study.

Matter of fact, I love to carry my **DEVOTION EXPLOSION!** notebook into small group Bible studies with me, just to liven things up. I like to wait until the leader smiles in relief, thinking he's made it through an entire evening without being embarrassed and says, "Well, if there are no other comments or questions . . ." And then I casually flip open the cover. I know, I know. I'm awful.

For an example of what a typical entry might look like, turn to page 100, and peek in on the little chat I had with the Lord about 1 Kings 22.

A parting word to the wise. You have absolutely no guarantee that the Holy Spirit is going to limit your explosions to one a day.

I remember the time when all I intended to do was write out a single page of Scripture and go straight to prayer. I didn't come right out and say it, but God, who can read a mind as easily as the back of a cereal box, knew perfectly well what I was thinking: *Man, is my schedule tight this morning! I shouldn't have slept so late. I sure hope my quiet time stays quiet today.*

Never, *ever* let your mind set you up with a blasphemous thought pattern like that one. It gets God's dander up.

You guessed it. All three—a "Wow!" a "Hmmm!" and a "Huh-oh!"—hit one right after the other.

"Incoming!" my brain screamed, but it was too late. Before I could slam my Bible shut and leap into a foxhole, the first one blew. My ears were still ringing when the second one exploded. I was staggering out on the battlefield, my fatigues hanging in tatters, when the third insight detonated in a blinding flash of light, leaving me spiritually shell-shocked.

I think I would have been all right, if it had been three "Wows!" three "Hmmms!" or even some challenging combination of just those two. But those "Huh-ohs!" just kill me, especially coming on the heels of the first two.

Best I can recall, I was on Psalms I.V.s for a week before they let me out of Intensive Care. Given today's harsh insurance restrictions, that's sayin' something.

One more piece of advice. When you go into that store for your notebook, pick out a fat one.

▼

High-Tech Prayer Trek

Ready for a prayer paradigm shift? Fasten your seatbelt. Here goes:

1. Open a password file in your computer and label it "Prayer."

2. Begin your prayer by addressing God as you want to experience Him today.

3. Forget subject quotas, proper wording, and every other stifling restriction—pour out your feelings, requests, confessions, thoughts, fears, obsessions, and desires, in any old order, just as they tumble out of your brain.

4. Observe three rules:

▼   Be yourself.

▼   Be totally honest.

▼   Be alert for what God wants to say to you.

5. Pray 'til the "ache" goes away or until you run out of time.

6. Delete your prayer.

7. Save the empty file and open it again tomorrow.

Bet you're staring at the page you just read like a mule at a new gate. But things is gonna get better. Honest. Next chapter.

▼

14

Would you be willing to pray on a donkey's jawbone?

If you're like most people, every time you try to pray for any length of time, your mind wanders.

In case you hadn't noticed, this probably doesn't do a whole lot for your relationship with God. What if somebody started talking to you, only to have his eyes glaze over in mid-sentence and say nothing for a couple of minutes? What if this happened again and again every time he tried to talk to you?

Would you look forward to your little chats together? Would you regard such a person as your dearest friend, or would you sooner or later draw the conclusion that you were far less important to him than the least little thing that happened to pop into his mind?

Are you ready to do something about it? If you are, I have the cure. But you're going to have to try to keep an open mind. I'm about to tell you how to pray by computer.

Does that sound too high-tech, too unspiritual? Maybe it is. On the other hand, it may turn out to be the most intimate, deeply spiritual thing you've done in your entire life.

So what if you don't own a computer? Does that mean you've just wasted the huge amount of money you spent on this book? Not at all. You can use your trusty old typewriter to pray too—manual or electric, makes no difference. For that matter, if you don't type, you can write out your prayers longhand. I'll briefly touch on alternative options a little later. But for now, since this is the way I learned to do it, I hope you'll humor me.

I admit that at first blush, a computer is an unlikely prayer facilitator. But please remember something important about God: He absolutely loves to use unlikely tools to accomplish His work. I'm convinced that's why He chose a mess like me to be a pastor.

To all my detractors—and I have many—I say, "I agree. Far too often, I'm a poor excuse for a Christian, let alone a pastor."

My personal opinion is that one day Satan was having a big laugh over my pathetic life, and God, wanting to demonstrate His sovereignty and power, called me into His service just to prove that He could do it.

In fact, based on 1 Corinthians 1:26–31, which reveals God's proclivity for choosing mostly fool-ish, weak, and lowly types to be His children, you probably weren't much when God called you either.

You would have to agree that the jawbone of a donkey is a pretty unlikely battle weapon. But Samson did manage to kill a thousand Philistines with one (Judg. 15:15). Don't you imagine that the same Lord who did that might be able to use a simple computer to defeat your nagging enemy of an unfocused mind in prayer?

Let me give you my testimony.

Five to seven days a week, nearly fifty-two weeks a year, I use my computer to pray. Most times, I pray at least two pages a day—that's thirty-eight single-spaced lines. Sometimes it's two, three, four, or five pages. One day I became so enthralled by the running conversation I got into with God on my computer that I ended up pouring out more than forty pages to Him over a period of eighteen hours.

But you don't need to get that carried away to make this powerful tool work wonders for your prayer life. If your mind frequently wanders while you're trying to talk to God, just five minutes of computer prayer may equal as much as a half-hour of what you've been used to.

How is that possible?

I used to be the all-time champion when it came to a wandering mind during prayer. I'd set out to pray for, say, five minutes, or maybe a half-hour, but I'd no sooner get started, than my mind would take off like a jackrabbit.

For example, I'd start to pray, "God, I really need Your help as I conduct this meeting coming up at 10:00 A.M. . . . " And that would be it. Without realizing it, I would automatically stop praying and start picturing how I might respond to various scenarios that could arise during the course of the meeting.

Five to ten minutes later, I'd come to my senses with the sudden realization of what I had done. "God, I'm sorry," I'd say. Then, trying to get back on track, I might plunge ahead by mentioning someone's name in prayer. "Lord, please heal Terry's marriage . . . " I'd begin.

But you guessed it. Same thing. For the next minute or two, my mind would be flooded with memories of when I had first met Terry and Ellen, what I perceived their relationship problems to be, what a devastating impact their impending breakup would have on their junior-high son Kerry, and on and on.

How defeating this was! Out of a half-hour I had set aside to pray, I might get only five or ten minutes of pure praying done. It was emotionally unsatisfying and guilt-producing, not to mention spiritually ineffective.

And then one day while sitting at my computer, it occurred to me that I hadn't devoted any serious time to God in prayer for quite a while. That made me feel guilty. But the trouble was, I was emotionally set to write, not pray.

Fingers on my keyboard, caught between duty and desire, I suddenly typed something like this:

God, I'm in the mood to write—but I know that You and I really need to talk. Would You mind if I prayed to You like this, today?

To begin with, I want to apologize for not talking with You lately. I've been busy serving You, sure. But I know You want more than my labor. You want me. And the truth is, I want You! O God! I really do. I want You!

You've been so good to me! You've . . .

Line after line after line I typed. About two pages into my prayer, it dawned on me. My mind hadn't wandered once! Somehow, the physical activity of my fingers flying across the keyboard coupled with watching the words of my prayer as they instantly appeared on the screen kept me intensely focused.

I checked my watch. A half-hour had gone by! I couldn't believe it. Where had the time gone? All too often, lately, just the reverse had been happening—thinking I had surely prayed a half-hour, I would look down to discover only five minutes had gone by.

Obviously, I was onto something here.

But there was something else too. This time, prayer had not seemed like an odious burden. It had been pure pleasure. It was not a "thing" I was doing to please God. I had actually been lost in intimate conversation with Him.

Since then, I have discovered that computer prayer is a kind of "prayer concentrate." I get at least as much real praying done on the computer in fifteen minutes as I previously got done in an hour.

For me, it's the perfect focusing agent. My mind doesn't stray. There's something about the experience of feeling my heart's cry to God move down from my mind, travel through my fingers, and materialize on the monitor before my eyes that creates a channel, a flow, a kind of stream of consciousness between me and my Creator. Sound familiar? It should—you're headed for another *DEVOTION EXPLOSION!*

Want to try? Sure you do. Read on.

. . . .

15

Open a vein-er-file in your computer and label it "prayer"

After you've learned to pray this way, you'll know why I call it opening a vein, instead of a mere computer file. You're about to learn how to pour out your life's blood, straight from your heart, to God.

This innocent-looking file becomes your rendezvous point with God. Yes, you could just open a new file each time, but you want this one to be special, sitting there among your other files, so you can see it and be reminded to pray every time you turn on your computer.

Since my files are arranged alphabetically, I've labeled mine "Aprayer," so it appears near the top. I like it handy when I'm ready for it. Its top position also reminds me that my prayer time with God is top priority in my life.

Additionally, I protect my prayer file with a password known only to me, so no one else can open it. Normally, I erase its contents each time I finish praying, for reasons I'll explain below. But sometimes my prayer time gets interrupted and I have to leave my computer in mid-sentence, hoping to return to it later. It's nice to know that all I have to do is close the file in the meantime, and my prayer will remain utterly private.

Why do I go to all that trouble to ensure complete privacy? Because I talk to God about everything. I mean *everything*. I bare my soul to Him, no holds barred. I wrestle through with Him the innermost secrets of my heart. I ask Him to rip away the facade and let me see my motives for what they really are. I confess my weaknesses, my lusts, my terrors, my anger with others, my dreams, my hopes and my highest desires.

When I pray, I am naked and defenseless before my Creator. If there was the slightest possibility that someone could break into my prayer file and read one of my half-finished prayers before I had a chance to delete it, my prayer time would become a charade, a farce, a mockery.

This ability to password-protect files is one reason I prefer computer prayer to typewriter prayer, unless you have instant access to a quality shredder. The same goes for longhand, with the additional drawback that because I'm a fast typist, longhand slows me down. When I try to write fast in longhand, I get writer's cramp. Now, if you're an accomplished speedwriter, or if you take shorthand . . .

16

Address God as you want to experience Him today

Did you ever think about the fact that the way you address someone can affect the course of the entire conversation? This is true even if you know the person extremely well.

When I telephone my wife during the day and begin the conversation with, "Judith Gayle, we've got to talk," you can pretty well count on this not turning out to be a lighthearted conversation.

When the first words out of my mouth, however, are, "Hi, Doll-Baby, watcha doin'?" she knows this is going to be one of those warm, cuddly check-ins she loves to receive when work tears us apart during the day.

I start our conversations in some even more interesting ways, but she won't let me tell you what those are.

And so it is in conversation with your dearest Friend in the whole wide world. Sometimes, when I'm desperate, I begin praying with a cryptic, "O My God!" At other times, I'm happy and mellow and start out with something like, "My Precious, Wonderful, Magnificent Lord!"

When I go to Him with a huge request, I've been known to open with, "Awesome God! Creator of the Universe! Omnipotent Majesty!" At other times, His triune nature is uppermost in my mind and I begin, "Father! Savior! Indweller!"

My point is this: Don't allow the first words of your prayer to become routine. As with anything else you do daily, if you don't take proper measures, you're liable to fall into a rut. And if you're doing it thoughtlessly, you ain't prayin'.

By varying the very first words of your prayers according to what's on your heart as you begin, you signal to your sleepy, preoccupied, or otherwise recalcitrant brain that this is different! This is vital! This prayer session is going to be unlike any other that has ever preceded it or will ever follow. Pay attention! Great starts make for great prayers.

17

Forget everything you've ever heard about proper prayer

Do you know a good formula for effective prayer? Forget it! From this moment forward I want to challenge you to pray limitless, unhampered prayers, guided only by what you have personally discovered is taught in the Bible itself.

Over the years I've watched preachers, writers, and missionaries put people in prayer straight-jackets. I've done it too. We didn't mean to, of course. We were just trying to help. And we did, a little. But after you've broken the prayer ice by using even the best formula, that's what you're left with, a formula.

God will put up with that for a little while. Hey, somethin's better than nothin', right? But sooner or later He's going to wince, if months later you're still trying to communicate with Him by formula.

I've researched the major prayers of the Bible. There *is* no formula. Everybody did it differently, depending on the personality of the pray-er and whatever was going on at the moment.

"What about the Lord's Prayer?" you may ask.

Jesus' disciples asked Him to show them how to pray, so He did. He gave them *a* way to pray. It works. I've used it countless times. Still do. But the Lord's Prayer isn't the only way to pray, nor even necessarily the best way, on all occasions.

Check out Jesus' prayer in John 17. Right in front of His disciples, He plunged into this awesome dialogue with the Father. Based on this prayer, you'd think He had never heard of the prayer He gave them in Matthew 6! Read the prayers of Jeremiah, Daniel, David, Peter, and Paul. They're all different!

You want to follow Jesus' prayer example? You want to pray with the greats, like the apostles and prophets? Then throw away the formulas. Be yourself. God will love you for it.

What if your best friend researched your personality and came up with a formula to be used in all future discussions with you? Would you be pleased? No you would not. As soon as you could see what was going on you would say, "Hey, forget the formula. This is me, remember? Just tell me what's on your mind. That's what I'm interested in."

"But I'm afraid my prayers won't be balanced!" you may nervously protest.

I hope they aren't. I hope your prayers are as unbalanced as real conversation. The other day my oldest son Pete called me long distance from Florida. "Did you see that?" were the first words out of his mouth.

He didn't have to explain. It was Sunday afternoon. The Dallas Cowboys were playing. Emmit Smith had just burst free for a thirty-yard touchdown romp. "Awesome!" I answered. "He cut through their defense like a hot knife through butter."

And we were off. For the next fifteen minutes we talked nothing but football. I didn't ask about Beth, Hunter, Jennifer, or Victoria. He didn't tell me he loved me or point out that I am the greatest father in the world. We didn't deal with the situation in the Middle East, global warming, or who would make the best president of the United States.

As best I can remember, I ended the conversation by saying, "Hey, Bud, I'm getting a call on the other line."

"No problem," he said. "Later."

And that was it. Unbalanced? You betcha. But he and I had a ball. This was father/son stuff at its best. No pretensions, no dancing around, no fancy rigmarole, just us, one-on-one, in the easy flow of our relationship, dealing exclusively with that moment in time.

Do we ever get around to all the other stuff? Sure. We have some heart-to-hearts like you wouldn't believe. Most times we do ask about other family members, catch up on personal news, share prayer requests, and express our love for one another. But not today. Why? Because when we're around each other, we're just ourselves. We've got nothin' to prove.

When it comes to lovemaking, your wife (or husband) probably doesn't want you to use a formula either. Now, a basic understanding of her anatomy and personality is real helpful, without a doubt. But if you slid into an invariable pattern of stroking her left arm for twenty seconds, gently kissing her left cheek for half-a-minute, nibbling at her right earlobe for twelve seconds, accelerating into two minutes of passionate kissing, then . . . she might interrupt this program with a special bulletin: "Oh, Sweetheart? Are you there? Great. So am I. I'll tell you what—tonight, surprise me, OK?"

Prayer is lovemaking with God. Dare to be creative. Dare to go where the two of you have never gone before. When you're alone with your God, let 'er rip. Ask the Holy Spirit to bring to your mind everything you and He ought to deal with during this session, and then trust Him to do exactly that. Dare to pour out your feelings, requests, confessions, thoughts, fears, obsessions, and desires, in any old order, just as they tumble out of your brain.

Know what? After one session like that, your heart, soul, and mind will be *on fire*. You'll never again want to return to the sterility of a formula.

And I'll tell you something else too. Once this kind of sky-soaring, heart-thumping, soul-searing prayer becomes the norm for you, no one will have to beat you up to make you say your prayers today. A hungry tyrannosaurus rex stationed in front of your computer terminal couldn't keep you away from another one of these unprogrammed, sky-diving, no-chute, free-fall plunges straight into the heart of God.

18

Cut the phony lingo

I'm on touchy ground here, but let me plunge in anyway: Have you fallen into the habit of speaking King James English during your prayers to God?

You are aware, aren't you, that the thees and thous, the wouldests and shouldests were words spoken by the average person in 1611, when the King James Version of the Bible was written? You are aware, aren't you, that Abraham, David, Peter, and Paul didn't use that kind of language when they talked to God? You are aware, aren't you, that the Bible was originally written in the common language of the people and that the only thing you're really doing when you pray like that is stumbling through a rather poor imitation of the way people talked four hundred years ago?

Now, let me hasten to say this: *If it works for you, keep doing it.* But let me hasten just as quickly to recommend that you *evaluate* whether or not it works as well as you think it does.

If someone strode into my office spouting, "O, thou most wonderful Stephen! I beseech thee, as I come into thy presence, to grant this, thy humble servant's wish . . ." I would be tempted to pick up the phone and call the men in white coats.

Frankly, who wants to be talked to like that? God doesn't need it unless you do. Jesus didn't talk to the Father like that. He used the common language of His day. And so should you—unless you know for sure that you can be absolutely real, honest, and transparent with God while using the thees and thous.

You see, many people *can't* get real with God when they talk like that. Their use of archaic language removes them and their prayers from everyday reality. They move into a kind of pseudo, mumbo-jumbo substitute for true holiness that masks who they really are and blocks out who God really is, turning potential majesty into mere mockery.

Remember when King Saul gave David his armor in a vain attempt to help the young warrior fight Goliath? It was a disaster! Saul's huge, thick, heavy armor worked fine for Saul, but the smaller David needed the complete freedom of movement necessary to whirl his sling over his head and send a

smooth stone sailing straight for the giant's unpro-
tected forehead. If David had attempted to meet the
enemy wearing Saul's cumbersome stuff, it would
have been David who lost his head, not Goliath.

All I want to do is help you be sure you're
using your sling. At least do what David did. He
tried on Saul's armor and found it was not for
him. So humor me, as David did Saul, and try
praying a time or two in everyday language, just
as you would talk to your best friend. Jesus *is*
your Best Friend.

If my suggestion to use everyday language
proves a hindrance to you, then cast it off. I'm not
the Holy Spirit, and I'm not applying for the job.

But if you discover to your stunned amazement
that praying to God in everyday language increases
your intimacy with Him and makes your prayer
sessions much more real, you may need to ask
yourself if perhaps, for all these years, King James'
English has been nothing more to you than King
Saul's armor.

19

Be alert for what God wants to say back to you

How does God get a word in edgewise, in this
high-tech, super-concentrated form of intense
prayer? Easy. He does it in the same three ways
anyone else would:

1. He waits for you to pause.

2. He interrupts you.

3. He answers your questions.

From time to time, even in the midst of a fingers-flying-over-the-keys prayer blitz, you'll pause, if only to work the kinks out of your weary digits. When you do, *listen.* If a thought pops into your mind, do what Eli taught the future prophet Samuel to do as a young child.

Say, "Is that You, Lord? Talk to me!" Type out exactly what you believe God may be saying to you. Don't forget to run a Word check on it, according to 2 Corinthians 10:5b. If, after you take that thought "captive" you note that it is "obedient to Christ," you might just have a keeper.

God has no qualms about interrupting you in mid-sentence either. After all, He's God. He has a right to say whatever He wants, whenever He chooses.

You know that irritating feeling you get when you're trying to talk and somebody keeps trying to interject a comment? The next time you get that feeling during prayer, type it out and pull a Samuel: "Is that You, Lord?" If it passes the 2 Corinthians 10:5b test, listen—very carefully. God's a gentleman. He wouldn't interrupt you if it wasn't extremely important.

Finally, ask lots of questions during prayer. Then listen for God's answers, typing them out and applying the Samuel question coupled with 2 Corinthians 10:5b.

Do these three things and in short order you'll discover that God knows how to use a computer too.

20

Pray 'til the "ache" goes away

Sometimes all you have is ten minutes to pray, and that's that.

But let me suggest a better way. As often as possible, put yourself in a position to pray for as long as it takes. I call it, "praying until the 'ache' goes away."

Several years ago I passed through the valley of the shadow of death in one extremely important area of my life. I was distraught beyond words. When alone, it wasn't at all unusual for me to break down, sobbing over what I perceived to be my terrible, irretrievable loss. It probably didn't help that, simultaneously, I was trying to get my money's worth out of a first-class mid-life crisis.

I would go to the Lord in prayer, feeling as though there was a knot in my chest, a dense, heavy ache that made it nearly impossible to go on. I prayed into that ache, peeling it away like the layers of an onion, telling God exactly how I felt and what I feared. I kept praying and praying and praying, until I had totally emptied myself upon my God.

Let me tell you, that's casting your cares on the Lord (Ps. 55:22). You know what I found? He sustained me, just as He promised He would. The problem was still there, but at least for that moment, the ache was gone.

The good news is that God worked a miracle through that time of utter submission to Him and His will, and pulled a Job on me. Some time later,

He restored to me infinitely more in that very area than He had initially taken away.

But I never forgot that lesson. Now, I've learned to identify the "ache." It's always there—but it's not always in the form of intense sorrow.

Sometimes, there's a bubbling effervescence that I can't stop—and don't want to! It can be as simple as having a lot of important stuff on my mind to talk over with my Best Friend and refusing to quit until I've got it all off my chest. At other times, it's an indefinable inner sense that, although I've finished my conscious agenda, some-how our conversation isn't complete. At such times I let my fingers pause over the keys, and wait.

The truth is, every single one of us has a deep, inner "ache" to know our Creator, our Savior, our Holy Indweller.

Give in to it.

21

Aaargh! You've got to delete it!

That's right, after all that praying, you've got to delete the contents of your file, then save the empty file and open it again tomorrow.

Why do you have to delete your written prayers? Because if you don't, you'll be tempted to save them for "posterity." Then you'll start "word-ing" your prayers to make them sound better when you reread them.

Or, even worse, God help your ambitious soul, you'll start entertaining the notion that you should pull your very best prayers into a collection for future publication. Once it enters your mind that somebody else may one day read your prayers, you're sunk. You can forget spontaneity. You will have prayed your last real prayer to God. From that moment forward, every word you type will be for *them,* not for Him.

You don't want your prayers polished and pretty. You want 'em real and ragged, just as they gushed out of your heart. So erase them. Every time.

However, if you find that by doing so, the blank page it leaves creates a kind of "prayer-writer's block" that makes it difficult for you to get started tomorrow morning, do this: Erase your entire prayer for today. Then type and save something like this:

"Tomorrow, Lord, I want to pray about the following:

1. Should I quit my job and find something else?

2. Do You want me to stay single for the rest of my life, or do You have someone in mind that You want me to marry?

3. What do You suggest I do to lose these forty extra pounds?"

When you call up your prayer file tomorrow morning and see a list like that, it should get you jump-started into fervent, fascinating, fruitful prayer quite nicely.

22

Prayer-prolonging procrastination power

Let's have a little chat about your area of greatest prayer guilt: the length of your prayers. I know, I know—you pray often. Sure you do. About a thimbleful. You try to reduce your guilt by clinging to Jesus' famous quote in Matthew 6:7: "And when you pray, do not keep on babbling like pagans, for they think they will be heard because of their many words."

That's sure not your problem, though, is it? In fact, if "many words" were required to be heard, your answers would come few and far between, wouldn't they—say, once a decade?

Plus, you're too smart to misuse the verse that way. For one thing, you can tell at a glance that rather than commanding that we pray only short prayers, Jesus is teaching against "babbling" or meaningless prayers. What's more, you know the kind of example Jesus Himself set: "One of those days Jesus went out to a mountainside to pray, and spent the night praying to God" (Luke 6:12).

And then there's that troubling verse in 1 Thessalonians 5:17 that tells us to "pray continually." Yeah, right. Something down deep tells you that a dozen sentence prayers scattered throughout the day might not exactly qualify for obedience to that command.

Truth be told, the passage that may best describe what Jesus would have to say about your

57

prayer life is Mark 14:37, when, in the Garden of Gethsemane, Jesus, who was facing imminent death, begged His disciples to watch and pray with Him: "Then he returned to his disciples and found them sleeping. 'Simon,' he said to Peter, 'are you asleep? Could you not keep watch for one hour?'"

No wonder few congregations sing the old hymn, "Sweet Hour of Prayer" anymore. Nobody in the church has a clue what the songwriter is talking about.

And yet, an hour of prayer *is* sweet. Indescribably so. At least once, before you shrivel up and die, you ought to try it. You probably already want to, if only to be able to say you actually did it. The question is, how?

Have I got a secret for you: Unleash the power of procrastination! All you have to do is to schedule an essential task you really despise—to begin right *after* you finish praying. Ha! You'll pray on and on!

Why, with that dreaded task waiting to attack as soon as you say, "Amen," you'll come up with prayer topics and depths of insight you never delved into before. Armed with this secret, people who have never been able to go beyond sixty consecutive seconds of prayer in their lives have been known to move into the sixty-minute category in their very first session.

You might even get to praying about how much you despise the task you're dreading. Having unloaded that emotional burden, you might dare to ask God to give you understanding into this dysfunctional part of your deviant personality.

God might actually show you how to crack the foundation of this stronghold in your life and beat it. Or He might grant you the wisdom to find the perfect person to whom you can delegate it. As a last-ditch deal, God might even send someone along to do this dreaded task for you while you're praying!

Who knows? It could happen.

If you pray long enough.

23

'Portant prayer postscript

Now you know how to experience a high-tech prayer trek. That's all there is to it—except for this postscript.

This is by no means my only form of prayer. Nor should it be yours. Remember what I said about getting stuck in a prayer formula.

Fact is, I still do more silent and verbal praying in my typical day than I do praying by computer. The good news is that after years of "computing" my prayers, my unruly mind has now been trained to stay more focused on God, no matter what form I use to communicate with my Best Friend.

As I said in chapter 14, if you don't have a computer you can employ most of these principles on your typewriter or by writing out your prayers in longhand. If you like, see what happens when you speak your prayers into a dictation machine!

Experiment. Be creative. As you adapt my suggestions to your own personality, I'm certain you will be able to improve on my approach.

So go ahead, cut me out of the loop. My feelings won't be hurt. When it's all said and done, it isn't about you and me. It's about you and God.

▼

P A R T 3

Maximum Memorization

Take a deep breath. Everything you ever detested about Scripture memorization is about to change.

1. Select a passage assigned to you by the Holy Spirit.

2. Write it out on several index cards, saying it aloud as you write it.

3. Place the index cards where you are likely to see them during the day.

4. When you're in the mood to do so, memorize the passage:

- ▼ Break up longer passages by memorizing them a verse at a time.

- ▼ Thoroughly absorb the verse's meaning.

- ▼ Say the verse aloud, including its reference before and after.

- ▼ Feel free to quit for the time being as soon as you can say the verse three times in a row without looking.

- ▼ Look for opportunities throughout the day to quote your new verse during conversa- .

tions with other people (and in spiritual warfare with Satan).

▼ Come back to the same verse each day until you can say it three times in a row without hesitating and without first having to refer to the card.

▼ Highlight the verse in your Bible.

5. Once memorized, add this verse to the previous verses you have memorized, making a list that you quote once a day.

6. When your list of verses grows so long that it feels too cumbersome to quote daily:

▼ ask the Holy Spirit to keep these verses hidden in your heart;

▼ ask Him to bring them to mind in the future every time you need them;

▼ stop your daily quoting of all the verses on your list—except the ones you just can't live without.

7. Begin a new list by memorizing the next verse—as soon as you get in the mood.

Sound similar to what you've heard before? That's because this is just a quick outline. What I'm about to do is to go to work on your *attitude* about Scripture memorization. Will you let me? Please? I'll be gentle. I promise.

▼

24

How'm I gonna memorize the Bible when I can't even remember my wife's name?

Nobody ever asks what my Ph.D. is in. If only they knew. Are you ready for this? I have a doctorate in Forgetfulness. So help me, it's the truth. Obtained it from Rotten Memory University.

Allow me to flash a couple of my credentials. Two months ago I rented a truck and drove my daughter, Tabitha, to college near Kansas City. On the way back I stopped for gas. Filled up, went in and paid, drove off.

Funny thing, though. As I was leaving, I could hear a strange sound behind me. Figured I must have run over something. Checked the rearview mirror and saw one of the attendants frantically waving his arms and jumping up and down. Was he yelling at me? I stopped the truck, climbed down, and walked back to see what his problem was.

I had forgotten to return the gas nozzle to the pump. There was the nozzle, still sticking out of my tank. Thirty feet behind the truck I could see the severed hose, whipping back and forth like a maniacal black snake, spewing gasoline all over the gas station lot.

With great dignity, I removed the decapitated nozzle from my tank, tiptoed around the rapidly-spreading lake of gasoline and carefully placed the nozzle on the nearest concrete island. As I quickly drove away from the scene and any potential explosion, I had to shake my head. What was this world coming to? I had thoughtfully taken the time to return the nozzle and the attendant had not even bothered to thank me.

Next credential. Three weeks ago on a Sunday morning, I was sitting in my office, just a-studyin' away. I was in the Word. I mean, I was *deep* in the Word. Someone tapped on my door.

"Come in," I said, wondering who would want to see me at this hour.

In walked Tim Hulsey, our head usher. "Uh, they're ready for you now."

"Who?" I said.

"The congregation."

I glanced at the clock on my desk. Oops. The service had started twenty minutes ago. "Are they singing the last song before I preach?"

"No," he said. "They finished that a couple of minutes ago."

I jumped to my feet, alarmed. "What are they doing, now?"

"Just waiting for you," he said.

"Oh, my God," I said, grabbing my Bible and racing toward the sanctuary. I wasn't using the Lord's name in vain. I had just uttered a very short but heartfelt prayer.

I slipped in the back of the sanctuary as quietly as possible and saw my minister of music, Teresa Patchin, desperately trying to fill the silence with an update on one of our missionaries.

As I clipped on my wireless mike, she spied me. "At last! He's here! Would you welcome to the pulpit, please—our pastor!"

As I strode down the aisle to the platform, the congregation applauded. Some pastors only merit applause when they preach an exceptional sermon. But my people know me and the special burdens I bear. I get an ovation just for showing up.

These are not isolated incidents. This is my life. Just ask my wife, Priscilla. I'd cite another forgetfulness credential, but right now I can't remember any more.

I tell you all of this so that you will be impressed with this next statement: In spite of my memory handicap, Judy and I have been able to memorize literally hundreds of Bible verses.

What's that? You don't believe me? OK, I'll prove it to you by quoting one of our favorite verses: "Do not let any unwholesome talk come out of your mouths, but only what is helpful for building others up according to their needs, that it may benefit those who listen" (Eph. 4:29).

See? I told you. Dead solid perfect. I nailed it, right down to the commas. If you don't believe me, look it up. Or ask my better half, Sherry. She memorized it too.

Now, what?

You think I cheated? You think I opened my Bible and peeked? How dare you cast aspersions on my . . . OK, OK, maybe I did. Perhaps I was just a tad nervous about getting it perfect.

Give me another chance, OK? I promise; this time I won't look. And I'll pick a hard one too. How hard? As hard as they come, John 3:16: For God so loved the world that he gave his one and only Son, that whoever believes in him enough to tithe and give offerings shall not only go to heaven, but be given a brand new Porsche to drive on those golden streets when he gets there.

I didn't look this time. Cross my heart! I didn't even ask Maud, my marvelous mate, to help me.

In fact, I quote this one to my congregation all the time—right before the offering. Are you convinced that my Scripture memorization plan works? Now that we've settled this little issue, *Mr. Doubting Thomas*, may I please continue?

The next five chapters are based on five Scriptures that will provide you with all the red-hot motivation and insider's techniques you will ever need to commit the Word of God to memory.

At least that's what my wife, Jane, said to tell you.

25

Scripture memorization helps you stop the bad stuff

*I have hidden your word in my heart
that I might not sin against you.*
Psalm 119:11

Because of the depth of our depravity, Judy and I fight daily battles against sinful thoughts, words, and deeds. We've learned that the Word of God is a powerful weapon in this life-or-death spiritual warfare.

However, when Satan slithers up with one of his insidious temptations, there's seldom opportunity for us to say, "Time out! Let me jump in the van, drive home, haul out my concordance, locate a couple of choice verses that speak to this temptation, and read them off to you. It will only take an hour or so for me to get ready to do battle with you, Beelzebub. Meanwhile, no fair hitting!"

We've just never had much success with that approach. Bet you haven't either.

The Psalm 119:11 strategy of hiding God's Word in your heart, through memorization, is God's answer to this dilemma. Every verse you commit to memory is a spiritual implement of war that you have lifted out of your weapons cache and hung on your belt. From that moment forward it's with you everywhere you go, twenty-four hours a day.

When one of Satan's demonic thoughts leaps out in surprise attack, all you have to do is reach for your belt, select the perfect weapon and, in the power of the Holy Spirit, cut the attacker to bits!

You can see it, can't you? You've *got* to have this instant protection.

26

Scripture memorization forces you to get it

When anyone hears the message
about the kingdom and does not understand it,
the evil one comes and snatches away
what was sown in his heart.
Matthew 13:19

Do you really hear what Jesus is saying in this verse? All the Bible reading in the world isn't going to help you one whit unless you understand it. True, writing out the Word as I'm urging you to do probably doubles your understanding of what you read. Speaking the Word out loud as you write it may double it again.

But why stop with a double-double? There's another level. Did I say "another level"? Let me rephrase that. We're talking a whole 'nother dimension, here.

Memorization *forces* you to understand the passage you've selected to memorize. Otherwise, it just won't stick. Sure, you can hang on to a few words by rote, saying the verse over and over and over again until it finally wears a shallow "groove" in your brain—but that's all. Without understanding, the rest of the verse will be as hard to hang on to as a hyper tot in a toy store.

Besides, rote memorization takes too long. You'll quickly discover that by far the fastest way to commit a verse to memory is to fall in love with it by thoroughly understanding it, backwards and forwards. As soon as you do—bang! It's in there. It'll flow like melted butter.

In fact, when you find yourself saying the verse over and over and you still can't remember it, nine times out of ten it will be because you haven't yet really reached in and grabbed its meaning.

When this happens, tell the Lord about it. Say, "Holy Spirit, I'm not *getting* this. You're the One who gave this passage to Paul; please give it to *me!* I want to love it and understand it, all the way to the marrow of my bones!"

Oh, does God love that kind of prayer, when you really mean it! And oh, will the understanding come—in His way and in His time, of course— but we're talking some serious sweetness, when that light finally goes on. I get goose bumps just thinking about those times when God has gladly pulled the scales from my eyes and let me see the power secreted away in one of His prime passages. Wow.

27

Scripture memorization helps keep you from becoming a spiritual dropout

The seed on good soil stands for those with a noble and good heart, who hear the word, retain it, and by persevering produce a crop.
Luke 8:15

This verse comes at the close of Jesus' explanation of the parable of the sower. In the verses just preceding, He makes it clear that lots of people who merely hear the Word end up dropping out.

But who hangs in there and really *does* something with her Christian walk? It's the woman who *retains* the Word she hears. By very definition, that's what Scripture memorization is: *retaining* the Word of God.

So memorize away and hang in there. What will be your reward? Second Timothy 2:12 is all the incentive I need: "If we endure, we will also reign with him."

28

You've already got a head start!

*"The word is near you; it is in your mouth
and in your heart."*
Romans 10:8

It's hard to tackle a verse cold and try to memorize it. But that's not what you're going to do during your *DEVOTION EXPLOSION!* You're going to be speaking it aloud as you write it out.

As this verse in Romans reveals, having God's Word in your mouth brings it near. Experience has taught me that when a Scripture is that near, I can reach out and put it in my heart through memorization—*which brings God's Word nearer yet.*

29

Build your day around your verse

These commandments that I give you today are to be upon your hearts. Impress them on your children. Talk about them when you sit at home and when you walk along the road, when you lie down and when you get up. Tie them as symbols on your hands and bind them on your foreheads. Write them on the doorframes of your houses and on your gates.
Deuteronomy 6:6–9

This passage is not some musty, dusty leftover from yesteryear, you know. The concept God reveals to His people here is critically important to anyone who wants to do more than give mere lip service to God.

. . . .

You know as well as I do that in this life there are talkers and there are doers. The talkers far outnumber the doers, but the doers far surpass the talkers when it comes to shaking this world for Jesus Christ.

Now, some people are doers because they're born and raised that way. As children, they always did their homework, made their beds, and ate their lima beans. As adults, they remember all birthdays down to the level of third cousins who live in Bangor, Maine. They pay their bills ten days early, and rake their leaves before spring. Thank God for these people. Without them, society as we know it would jump the track and end up in the bottom of some nasty ravine.

I, alas, cannot count myself among their exalted number. I hid my lima beans in my napkin, saw no point in making my bed since I was just going to have to unmake it again at night, and went on a one-kid crusade against homework from kindergarten through my undergraduate years in college.

If anybody we owe gets paid on time, they have my wife to thank. People from my church have been known to take pity on my longsuffering spouse by coming over and raking our leaves for us. And if anybody we know gets a birthday, anniversary, Christmas, or Groundhog Day card, once again, they have my wife to thank (although, somewhat miraculously, I do manage to remember my wife's special days. Given the degree to which I lean on her, I can't afford to lose this precious woman).

Shamefully, I must admit that I belong to that disgraceful mass of terrible slackers who will never amount to a hill of beans (lima or otherwise) unless we come up with some sort of secret to totally transform deficient character.

Now, admittedly, I have a long way to go. But lest you think this passage hasn't been doing me any good, allow me to point out that as of the date this book went to press, I have still, by the grace of God, managed to stay out of prison. Given the total depravity with which I daily wrestle, that's saying something.

So what does this passage have to do with maximum memorization and character transformation? It helps you burn God's truth into your heart and then move it into your public persona, that's what. Actually, I've found that an encounter with God, closely followed by the loss of my closet Christian status, has been quite beneficial in keeping me on the straight and narrow. I suspect you could use the help as well.

I recommend implementing this Scripture passage in three phases, which I will describe in the next three chapters.

30

The capture phase

Starting this very moment, be constantly on the lookout for those Scripture passages the Holy Spirit highlights for you to memorize. You'll know which ones they are.

One passage may leap out at you while you're listening to your pastor's sermon or participating in your small group Bible study. Another may hit you between the eyes while you're reading a Christian book, listening to a Christian music CD, or absorbing the Bible on cassette. If your experience is anything like mine, most of the time it will happen in a *DEVOTION EXPLOSION!*—while you're writing out the Word in your one-on-one time with God.

As soon as you capture a hot verse, write it out on several index cards. Caution: Don't make the mistake of typing it to make your cards look all nice and neat. You want this critically important passage to be in your own printing or handwriting.

Typing may be easier to read at a glance, but remember: Scripture memorization is hiding God's Word in your heart. So what does that make this? Open heart surgery! Your brain will be far less likely to reject the Scripture transplant when it instantly recognizes your handwriting on the cards as its own.

31

The placement phase

To get the Word of God into our hearts our text tells us to, "Tie them as symbols on your hands and bind them on your foreheads. Write them on the doorframes of your houses and on your gates" (Deut. 6:8–9). In other words, find a way to position God's commands so that you are reminded of them everywhere you go, all day long.

Why? Because if Satan can't stop you from having any exposure to the Word, he has a fallback plan. "At least," he says, "let's keep this thing contained within your devotional time. I'll concede that I've lost those thirty minutes. But the other twenty-three-and-a-half hours are mine!"

You can't take that lying down. You dare not call a timeout and recline even so much as a single moment of a single day in Lucifer's lair. You've got to let the fire of God blaze hot in your eyes and growl, "Wrong, Satan. This is the day the Lord has made. Every single minute of every single hour belongs to my Jesus. And to remind myself of that, I'm going to destroy your containment strategy with a breakout plan that keeps my relationship with Him going strong, all day long."

Think of the Scripture index cards you have prepared as land mines that have the power to trigger a **DEVOTION EXPLOSION!** The difference is, these are mines that you *want* to step on! What you want to do is set these little babies to go off wherever you know you are likely to catch a few moments of available brain time during the day.

Some very nice in-your-face places are: clipped to a corner of the computer screen; propped above the kitchen sink; taped to the bathroom mirror; posted on the dash of the van; slipped into a shirt pocket; used as a Bible/book marker—the list is endless.

How do you trigger them? Simple. Let's say you're in your car, headed home on the interstate after an exhausting day at work. You can't wait to get out of your suit, grab a shower, and unwind.

Suddenly, traffic slows to a crawl. Way in the distance you can see flashing red and blue lights. There's been an accident. Oh, great. You hit your brakes, then smack the steering wheel with both palms in frustration.

Taking a deep breath, you start pushing buttons on your radio, trying to find something decent to listen to. But there's nothing on except commercials, elevator music, and that one stupid song they keep playing that you absolutely hate. Giving up on the radio, you hit the "off" button and your hand brushes the index card on your dash, knocking it to the floor.

You lean down, pick up the card, and prop it back up on the dash. As you do, you glance at your own handwriting at the top: "Chill out with James 1:20!"

In spite of yourself, you smile. You know yourself so well, choosing the "Chill Out" card for the car. *OK, Jesus,* you think, *hit me with Your best shot.* And then you read: "Man's anger does not bring about the righteous life that God desires."

BOOOOM!

You've just triggered a **DEVOTION EXPLOSION!**

You gaze out the window, mind racing, letting the power of God's Word sink into your heart. You're ready. And using step 4 from the "Maximum Memorization" chapter, you begin to memorize James 1:20.

32

The game

I know your brain. In spite of all the benefits we've listed, it's still scared. Scripture memorization is tough. And Satan fights it with everything he's got.

To coax your mopey mind into maximum memorization, you need to be wise as a snake and harmless as a dove. In other words, you're gonna have to lighten up, wipe that self-righteous scowl off your face, and make this thing fun!

I just happen to have a little game you can play. Not only will it help you fix in mind the Scriptures you are memorizing, but it will transform you into an excellent biblical witness throughout the day.

Object of the game: Take the verse you are currently trying to memorize and work it into as many conversations as possible during the course of your day.

To work a verse into a conversation, of course, you need an opening. Ah, but Openings R Us! Let's take Proverbs 16:9 as an example: "In his heart a man plans his course, but the LORD determines his steps."

Responding to Openings. An example of how to do it this way would be someone who point-blank asks you, "Do you think you can accomplish anything you want, so long as you can come up with the right plan?"

You blink once, twice, then, stunned that you actually have a biblical response, you stammer,

"Ah, well, actually, you know, the Bible says—just a minute, let me think—uh, no, wait a minute, I've got it, I've got it—Proverbs 16:9! 'In his heart a man plans his course, but the LORD determines his steps.'"

Watching for Openings. In this case, you've got your hand on your Scripture, the way a gunslinger lightly brushes his fingers across the grip of his holstered Smith & Wesson. You're ready to draw.

Suddenly, the person you're with makes his move. " . . . and I just couldn't believe it. Down the tubes, after all that planning."

There's the "whissssk!" of emptied leather and a blur of sunlight glinting off metal barrel. "I hear you. Just this morning I was reading in Proverbs, 'In his heart a man plans his course, but the LORD determines his steps.'"

Notch that baby.

Creating Openings. "Congratulations!" you're saying to your newly promoted coworker. "You really worked hard for this. Solomon—the wisest guy who ever lived—once said, 'In his heart a man plans his course, but the LORD determines his steps.' You know what that's tellin' me? The Big Guy's smiling on you. No doubt."

Stealth Openings. Face it. Some people you're with just can't handle hearing the address. They're open to truth, so long as they don't know it comes from the Bible. So don't tell 'em. Biblical truth works, regardless. No way is God's Word gonna return void.

You seize your opening and comment with a shrug, "Hey, you know what they say—'In his heart a man plans his course, but the LORD determines his steps.'" Then sagely nod. No further comment. No need. It's in there.

At the end of the day, add up how many times you managed to quote your verse while engaged in conversation with other people.

As a sort of goad and guide, here's some Gospel of Luke Scoring:

0 times: Judas Chicken (22:1–6)
1 time: Rich Young Ruler Courage (18:18–25)
2 times: Zacchaeus Courage (19:1–10)
3 times: Persistent Widow Courage (18:1–8)
4 times: Woman Who Anointed Jesus' Feet Courage (7:36–50)
5 times: Joseph of Arimathea Courage (23:50–53).

33

What's this deal about not having to memorize Scripture until I'm in the mood?

Don't think I don't know what you're thinking. You're probably wondering how I'm going to make this recommendation without sounding like one of those wishy-washy people who don't believe in standards or discipline.

Well, I don't blame you. If we waited to do all the things we're supposed to do until we were in the mood, there would be a whole buncha things—important things—that would go undone.

On th'other hand, memorization is a tricky thang. There's something about our brains that makes 'em get downright antsy when we suddenly inform them that they're going to have to make room somewhere in all that convoluted gray stuff for a piece of information that we, uh, well . . . that we want to remember . . . forever? It would be kinda like going home and announcing to your household that someone is coming over tonight.

"We're having somebody over for dinner?" you might get asked.

"Well, no," you reply. "Actually, they're going to stay."

"You mean overnight?"

"No, I would say a bit longer than that."

"So how long is this house guest going to mooch off of us?"

"Try substituting 'permanent resident' for 'house guest' and you'll begin to get the idea."

"But, but, that will disrupt our lives! Besides, we don't have room for a permanent house guest. There's no place to put him!"

"Then we'll just have to take out a construction loan from the bank and build on. I want him to stay."

"Fine. You want somebody else to live here? No problem. In fact, he can have my room. Know why? Because I'm leaving!" Door slams.

Maybe other people's brains don't regard memorization as that big a threat. But mine does. The moment I even consider bringing in a new boarder, my brain throws itself on the floor, kicking and screaming, "I won't! I won't! I won't!"

And that goes double when it's Bible memorization. Why? We're talking spiritual warfare, that's why. For all the reasons I've been giving you, Satan fears and despises the hiding of God's Word in my heart. When I try to bring my new "permanent Scripture resident" inside, the devil starts lobbing grenades through the windows.

My brain doesn't like grenades. They tend to increase the amount of mental housecleaning that needs to be done after a satanic attack. When the first few come crashing through the panes of glass, pins pulled and spinning across the floor, it gets downright pitiful inside my skull.

Terror-stricken, my brain gets down on its squishy knees and fervently pleads with me, "Please don't memorize Scripture! It's not worth it! I'll do anything, if you only reconsider. I'm begging you!

"Tell you what," my brain continues, "next time your wife has a last-minute cooking emergency and sends you to the store for flour, milk, and eggs, I'll remember all three, honest! It won't be like last time when she burst into tears because you came back with avocados, underarm deodorant, and a nifty computer magazine."

Brains. Can't live with 'em, can't live without 'em. What are you gonna do? And I'll tell you something else. Brains don't get any easier to live with over the years. The older my brain gets, the harder it fights having to memorize anything.

So what's a wanna-be spiritual giant to do?

34

You gotta sweet-talk your brain

How do you sweet-talk a brain? It goes something like this:

"Darling, snookums, baby, honey-bunch, I was just thinking. Do you suppose we might have Micah 7:7–8 over to visit some evening—not right away, oh, no, no, no. Heaven's-to-Betsy, no! I wouldn't dream of doing that to you, what with all you're trying to keep track of, right now. But I mean, some day. Just for a minute or two. Just to meet him.

"He's such a good Scripture. I know you'll fall in love with him! Besides, he's so handy to have around during one of those nasty satanic attacks you despise. Do you know he can grab a grenade off the floor and throw it right back out the window before it explodes?

"And then, if you really like him, maybe sometime he can come back for supper. Who knows? You might get to liking him so much that you might be tempted to ask him to stay!

"But let's not talk about that right now. For the moment, all I ask is that you think about it. I'll just jot down the number where he can be reached, at the bottom of this page of Scripture I've been writing out. I might even scatter his address around in some of the places we visit during the day, just so we don't forget that he's there. Then, when you get in the mood to have some additional help around here with all the hard work you do, just let me know, and we'll invite him right over!"

Are you beginning to get the idea? A little respect for what your brain can and can't handle on any given day goes a long way. You treat your brain right and it will repay you a hundredfold.

35

You want Scriptures? I've got 'em!

Huh? What's that, you say? You want biblical permission to memorize Scripture when you feel like it? I was afraid you would never ask. Through Solomon, the wisest man (until Jesus) who ever lived, the Holy Spirit reminds us: "There is a time for everything, and a season for every activity under heaven" (Eccles. 3:1).

There are no exceptions to this immutable law of God. Go ahead. Set out your tomato plants in January, when it's twelve below. But don't plan on a BLT sandwich anytime soon. You planted out of season.

So it is with Scripture memorization. There is a time, a season, when your brain is fertile and ready for the next implantation. Respect that fact and be ready when your brain gives you the go-ahead.

Using the *DEVOTION EXPLOSION!* approach will result in fewer Scriptures memorized, at first. At one time or another in our Christian lives, most

Christians have succumbed to duty, assignment, or guilt and have gone on a memorization binge. That's all well and good. No matter how you get the Word of God in there, the fruit of having done so is marvelous.

But very few people who force memorization continue. A month or two after starting, they're so exhausted by the emotional effort of chiseling into frozen January soil that they give up.

By contrast, respecting the Holy Spirit's timing and prompting enables you to make Scripture memorization a fulfilling, rewarding way of life. So what if you only add a verse or two to your list in a week or a month? If you're still memorizing Scripture ten years from now, you'll be light-years ahead of the start-and-stop crowd.

But that's not all God has to teach us through Solomon. Listen to this same principle in beautiful lyrical terms: "Do not arouse or awaken love until it so desires" (Song of Songs 2:7).

Always remember: Scripture memorization is not some cold, calculated, cerebral activity. It's a lover's decision. It springs from your passionate, unbridled love for Jesus Christ and your desperate desire to please and be like the One who loved you so much that He died for you.

The psalmist didn't write, "I have hidden your word in my head that I might not sin against you." He wrote with tender devotion, "I have hidden your word in my *heart*" (Ps. 119:11).

It is your love for your Lord and Savior that melts all resistance to Scripture memorization and causes you to welcome the permanent residency of His Word, implanted deeply within your heart. True lovers seldom force themselves on one another. They wait until the moment is right. When it arrives, they always know.

And so will you.

▼

PART 4

Oddities
and
Essentials

36

The five-minute Devotion Explosion!

Trust me. The Devotion Police will come after me with tires screeching and sirens blaring for having the audacity to write this chapter.

The very idea—not only suggesting to backsliders that it's OK to spend a mere five minutes with God, but coming up with a nifty plan to help them do it! But I gotta. I can't help it; I'm a realist.

Maybe you're not ready to be a two-hour-a-day-Paul's-journeys-along-dusty-roads scholar. Maybe you're one of those precious newcomers to this whole devotions scene whom Jesus loved so much that it cost Him His life. Maybe you could use something bite-sized to begin with, to let you ease into this thing, like lowering your shivering body into a hot bath.

Maybe, before you take the plunge, you just need to get your feet wet.

But the truth is, even those of us who would love to spend an hour or more with the Lord sometimes oversleep or get totally overcommitted for a day or a week or a month.

When that happens to you, I don't want you to skip your devotions. I want you to have a shortened version, ready and waiting, that you can pull out, employ and enjoy, at a moment's notice.

Think of this chapter as you would a health food bar or a chocolate-flavored nutrition shake. It's definitely not as satisfying as a full-course devotional meal, but it is loaded with essential vitamins that you don't want to try to get through your day without. Better something than nothing.

And I happen to know something that even the Devotion Police would have to agree with, in spite of themselves: Five minutes with God beats a year with anybody else.

Besides, this isn't just any old haphazard, five-minute devotion. This is **DEVOTION EXPLOSION!** A single dose of this stuff is so concentrated, so potent, that it can revolutionize your day.

Are you ready? Take a deep breath and let's go:

1. Turn on your computer.

2. While it's booting up, take out your **DEVOTION EXPLOSION!** Scripture page and write out the first three verses of the Book of Proverbs. (Save the next three verses for tomorrow, and so forth.)

3. Turn to your **DEVOTION EXPLOSION!** notebook and make a sixty-second entry under "Hmmm!" "Huh-oh!" or "Wow!" depending on where it best fits. Your entry should try for a soul-stripping reply to this question: *What do I think God is saying to me through this passage that I should immediately apply to my life?*

4. Click open your password-protected file marked "Prayer" and pour out your heart to God as fast as you can type, about whatever pops into

your mind. Trust the Holy Spirit to guide you, and He will.

5. When the five minutes are up, quit.

I guarantee you: Number Five will be the step you have the most trouble following.

Now the obligatory spiritual health warning: *Yes, you can use the Five-Minute **DEVOTION EXPLOSION!** to survive, for a while. But is that all you want to do? Merely survive? Wouldn't you rather thrive? Longterm, it's going to take just a tad more commitment from you than a mere five minutes of your precious time each day.*

37

When you experience burnout

If you're the kind of person who has eaten raisin bran cereal for breakfast every morning for the past ten years and eagerly anticipate enjoying a hearty breakfast of raisin bran cereal for ten years to come, you can skip this chapter. You have absolutely no need for it.

But if your spouse has fed you five different kinds of cereal on Monday through Friday of this week, and you think you will scream if you don't have something besides cereal for Saturday breakfast, you've come to da right place.

I wrote **DEVOTION EXPLOSION!** especially for you. You're absolutely gonna love my system. For a while. But in a week or a month or a quarter you're gonna burn out. Always before, that's meant that you quit doing daily devotions for a week or a month or a quarter or longer.

But not this time. You're gonna outsmart the burnout factor, see. And your daily devotions are gonna stay right on course. How? By varying the way you experience God each day, according to your need. Anyway you choose.

Your variety requirement may be so high that you need to find seven systems, one for each day of the week. In that case, **DEVOTION EXPLOSION!** will be one of the seven.

On the other hand, you might like **DEVOTION EXPLOSION!** so well that you'll stay with it seven days a week for six months before you blow a gasket. What then? Be prepared. All the while **DEVOTION EXPLOSION!** is working for you, be on the lookout in your local Christian bookstore for an alternative system that sounds interesting.

When you finally hit the wall, take a break from **DEVOTION EXPLOSION!** and go straight into the alternative you've lined up. Chances are, in a couple of weeks or months, your spiritual palate will be cleansed and you'll be ready to take a fresh run at **DEVOTION EXPLOSION!**

However, you may be more like me. Although I've done it several different ways, at this stage of my life, I find that **DEVOTION EXPLOSION!** perfectly meets my needs Monday through Friday. But come the weekend, I'm ready for a change.

What kind of a change? Here are some ideas:

Vary the Way You Pray

▼ Use a typewriter instead of a computer.

▼ Write your prayers out in longhand.

▼ Go somewhere alone and pray out loud.

▼ Set your alarm to go off a half-hour early and go for a brisk walk while you pray aloud.

▼ Pray into a tape recorder. When you're finished, play it back and then erase it.

▼ If you can do it with your eyes open, try praying aloud while you drive. Caution: this works best if you have the ability to put your car on automatic pilot while you focus in prayer. Otherwise, you could end up in the wrong place— or lost. Also, I highly recommend deeply-tinted windows. Without them, the people on either side of you during traffic jams are tempted to dial 911 on their cellular phones and report you as mentally unhinged.

Vary the Way You Write Out the Word

▼ If you've been writing out the Word at the kitchen table, change to a lap board in front of the fireplace in your living room. If it's not fireplace weather, take a lawn chair out under a tree.

▼ Do your devotions at a different time of the day.

▼ Change ink color as you write out the Word. I've used both blue and black. You may want to try red and green during December.

▼ Instead of writing out the Word on weekends, you might want to pull out your *DEVOTION EXPLOSION!* notebook and do a Bible study on one of your explosions that go "Hmmm!" "Huh-oh!" or "Wow!"

▼ Instead of typical devotions on Saturday, make

a weekly appointment to share with your spouse or a friend what you got from your **DEVOTION EXPLOSION!** during the past week. Sharing it aloud with someone else will increase your understanding and your appreciation for just how much blessing and sacred insight God has showered upon you during your awesome times of intimacy with Him in recent days.

Ask him to share what God has been showing him during his quiet time as well. If he doesn't have much to say when it's his turn, tell him to go out and buy his own copy of **DEVOTION EXPLOSION!** and get connected.

Do not loan him your copy, however. He may get so attached to it that you may never see it again.

38

The Messiah Complex

(Don't read this chapter. Not yet.
Wait until you've been praying so successfully
that you've built up a really long prayer list.
Then come back here and see me.
I'll help you.)

If Satan can't keep you from praying (Plan A), then he goes to Plan B, which is to try to keep you from praying effectively. So far in this book, I've shared with you my Bible strategies for dismantling both Satan Plan A and Satan Plan B.

But very few people know that Satan also has a Plan C—as in, Complex, Messiah.

What's a Messiah Complex? Well, it's akin to that attitude that descends upon some overweight people who have just managed to lose their first twenty pounds, in thirty days. Suddenly they are experts on rapid weight loss. They swiftly, harshly judge any rotund human they see who is not "doing something" about his or her problem.

Other than the fact that they're really obnoxious to be around, their biggest problem is that they have slipped into the dreaded "haughty spirit before a fall" syndrome that Solomon warned about (Prov. 16:18). They have forgotten that only thirty-one days before, they might have been every bit as gluttonous as the people they are now judging.

Now. Let's suppose that God really blesses *DEVOTION EXPLOSION!* in your life and you manage to put together thirty straight days of first-class one-on-one time with God. At that point, you're likely to feel spiritually stronger than you've ever before felt in your life.

What's more, in those thirty days, you'll probably have received some super insights, witnessed some really huge answers to prayer, and grown quite a prayer list as a result. When you start witnessing about all God is doing in your life, your friends, neighbors, and acquaintances will probably ask you to be sure to pray for them because right now, you're "where it's happening." They're not stupid. They'll all fight for a coveted place in your prayer life, right under "the spout where the glory comes out."

Naturally, in your newfound sense of spiritual power, you'll promise to pray for them. Even better, you *will* pray for them, just as you promised. And some of them will receive significant answers to prayer. Word will get out. Your prayer list will grow.

Before you know it, Plan C will be upon you. Splendidly robed in your full-length Messiah Complex, you will faithfully war on, in prayer, because if you don't do it, *it won't get done.*

At some point your prayer time will become uncomfortably long. Battling sleep deprivation, you'll set your alarm clock to get up earlier and earlier—or you'll stay up later and later, so you can slog through your list—which now includes the second cousin of somebody's aunt who used to know a person who graduated with the son of a woman in your wife's Tuesday small group. You have no idea what his name is or even, for that matter, if he's actually male, but the reference to this unknown person is here, nonetheless, right on your prayer list. Did I say prayer "list"? Make that prayer "book."

Prayer time is no longer fun. It's dry. It's hard. It's odious duty. You're starting to get grouchy. But you gotta do this thing, see. 'Cause God bless America, the whole shebang depends on spiritual giant you.

You've totally forgotten that a scant thirty-one days before, God somehow managed to keep the entire world spinning on its axis without so much as a how-de-doo from spiritual giant you.

A while back, one of my best buddies and most treasured prayer partners asked to see me. Plan C was all over him. "I don't know what to do," he confessed.

So I gave him my permission to remove his Superman cape and quit jumping off of high buildings. I also sprinkled a little pastoral holy dust on his harried head and gave him my blessing to ax 95 percent of his prayer list, trusting that somehow, the Lord would be able to locate, train, and anoint other prayer warriors who would take up the slack.

In exchange for this blessing, the only requirement I placed on him was that he double his prayer time for me. Just kidding. After a while, I checked back with him. The joy had returned to his prayer life.

Has Satan slipped Plan C in on you? If he has, it's time to deal with it. If you don't, he'll win. He knows that if this continues much longer, the pressure will build until you throw up your hands in despair and quit praying altogether.

Ready? Here it comes: *With all the powers vested in me as Grand Poo-Bah of the DEVOTION EXPLOSION! phenomenon, I hereby grant you official permission to remove your Superman cape and cease jumping off of tall buildings.*

Ahem. Bow your head, please.

Whooooooosh! Sprinkle-sprinkle-sprinkle.

Feel that pastoral holy dust settle on your harried head? It's good stuff, isn't it? My dad found it on sale in a little shop tucked away on a side street in the Old City, during his last trip to the Holy Land.

Let's see, where was I? Oh, yes: *I further hereby bestow upon you my blessing to ax 95 percent of your prayer list, trusting that somehow, the Lord will raise up and anoint many other prayer warriors who will be willing and able to take up the slack. May the freedom, exultation, and joy of your prayer life swiftly return.*

In exchange for this huge favor, my only requirement is that you must immediately add my name to your shortened prayer list.

I'm not joking.

39

There's no explosion if there's no encounter

DEVOTION EXPLOSION! is about one thing only: an encounter with God. Without the encounter, there's no explosion. It's just ho-hum devotions. It's just quiet time. Reeeeal quiet.

Whatever you do, don't approach writing out the Word, prayer, or Scripture memorization as ends in themselves. Don't expect them to "do it" for you. They can't. Anything like that sorry approach is going to leave you sorely disappointed.

"Stupid plan," you'll say. "That dumb DEVOTION EXPLOSION! didn't do nothin' for me." And you'll be right. But you'll also be left—out in the cold.

DEVOTION EXPLOSION! is not the room you want to enter. But it is a fairly decent door. And that's how you've got to use it if you want it to work.

Approach each DEVOTION EXPLOSION! ingredient—writing out the Word, typing your prayer, Scripture memorization—as a doorway you're going to step through into an awesome encounter with God.

Imagine yourself stepping across the threshold into the Holy of Holies of His presence. And then you realize that it's not your imagination. It's real. That's what Jesus' death on the cross bought you. You're a member of the family now.

Compared to God, I'm nothing. But as insignificant as I am, you'll probably have to call for an appointment if you want to get in to see me. (No, I don't know why anyone would want to do that, either, but stay with me on this one for a minute.)

When you arrive at the church I pastor, you'll walk up to the receptionist, announce that you have an appointment to see me, and be invited to have a seat in the waiting room. Then you'll wait while the receptionist calls back to my secretary, who will call into my office to tell me my three o'clock appointment has arrived. I may tell her, "Give me ten more minutes," while I try to reach closure with the person who came in before you. Finally, the receptionist will buzz you through the security door and my secretary will lead you through the catacombs to my office. She'll knock on the door and I'll say, "Come in!" And then we'll meet.

If my door is closed, even my staff members knock first, out of respect (I prefer to think that's why). But any day of the week, any time of the day, there are at least fourteen people who can walk in through the private door of my office unannounced, without an appointment, without knocking: Judy, Pete, Beth, Hunter, Jennifer, Victoria, Tab, Miley, Trey, Mileyah, Abi, Beki, Abe, and Ari. Why? Because they're my wife, kids, and grandkids, that's why. My typical response when one of them barges in on me like that is a smile, often followed by a big hug and a kiss.

You're God's kid. You can walk in on Him anytime and find a smile, a hug, and a kiss—and a whole lot more.

Through *DEVOTION EXPLOSION!* I've shared with you the location of one of the private doors that leads into God's office. Use it.

40

Seein' is believin'

I thought you might appreciate seeing some actual samples of the key elements in *DEVOTION EXPLOSION!* The next pages of this chapter are just that.

A Devotion Explosion! Scripture Memorization Land Mine

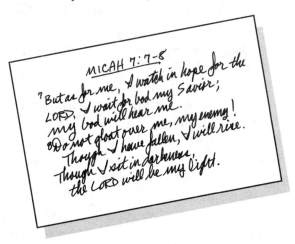

MICAH 7:7-8

7 But as for me, I watch in hope for the LORD, I wait for God my Savior; my God will hear me.
8 Do not gloat over me, my enemy! Though I have fallen, I will rise. Though I sit in darkness, the LORD will be my light.

The Devotion Explosion! Scripture Pages

Book __Romans__   Chapter __13__ Verse __14__ Date __9-9-99__

Scripture

Notes

14 "Rather, clothe yourselves with the Lord Jesus Christ, and do not think* about how to gratify the desires of the sinful nature.

think - 2 Co 10:5b

The Weak and the Strong

14 ¹ Accept him whose faith is weak*, without passing judgment on disputable matters. ² One man's faith allows him to eat everything,* but another man, whose faith is weak, eats only vegetables. ³ The man who eats everything must not look down* on him who does not, and the man who does not eat everything must not condemn the man who does, for God has accepted him. ⁴ Who are you to judge someone else's servant? To his own master he stands or falls. And he will stand*, for the Lord

weak - 2 Co 12:9-10

everything - 1 Co 6:12

down - 1 Pe 5:5b

stand - Eph 6:10-18

Memorize: Ro 14:1

Study: 14:1 - what is "disputable"?

☑ Quoted Scripture List ☑ Memorized new Scripture ☑ Wrote in commentary ☑ Prayed

34
Page

HMMM!

LYING SPIRITS

GOD'S METHODS

CHANCE OR DESIGN?

8-4-99, 6:18 a.M. — I Kings 22:19-23

— First of all, LORD, I believe what I just read. Furthermore, I trust You. But I've got to admit that I don't understand all the angels around You — is this a heavenly staff meeting? Okay, that I can handle.

But what is this? A brainstorming session? You know everything, including the thoughts of angels, so this can't be about Your being stumped for a good idea. So you have to be doing this for the sakes of the angels — but why? To train them?

Okay. For the sake of argument let's say You're training them. But training them how? To lie? To entice unsuspecting beings? All right, all right — that's a bad guy. A real bad guy. He has it coming. But why didn't You just send down a lightning bolt, if You wanted to do him in? Why entice him with a lie?

And while we're on the subject of lying... I thought Satan was the Father of all lies. Well, there's no "truth" to it. That's what You said, in John 8:44. You said lying is Satan's native language.

Now You, on the other hand, You're the truth! Isn't that what You declared, in John 14:6? So how do I reconcile that with this passage, which says, "So now the LORD has put a lying spirit in the mouths of all these prophets..."?

Does it not count when it's someone else who does it? Is this simply a function of warfare — as in "All's fair in love and war" — and therefore falls into a totally separate category? Or is this simply You proving Your sovereignty — that You can do what You please, when You please? (Romans 9:10-24)

Show me, LORD — in Your way and in Your time. Meanwhile, I trust You.

8-5-99 5:57 a.M. — I Kings 22:34

— Is there such a thing as a "random" event, LORD — especially

High-Tech Prayer Trek

Author of the Ages!

I love You!

I'm scared about this book, Lord. I've tried so hard to do it the way You want it done, but now that I'm this close to being finished, I'm aware of how helpless I am to get anything of any consequence done without Your blessing and favor.

And I'm really the one to be writing a book like this, huh? I am so sorry for my inconsiderate attitude with Judy and Ariel at lunch today. Here Judy called me, all lovey-dovey and wanting to spend some time with me, and all I could think about was this stupid book. Forgive me for grouching at traffic while I was trying to get out of McDonald's. Please forgive me for being so distracted that Judy had to repeat herself again and again. And then when she asked me what was wrong, I couldn't even admit that it was my fault. Please, please help me make it up to her tonight, Lord. My beautiful, precious, tender, hard-working wife deserves better than this. And so do You, from some guy who's supposed to be an example of how much it helps to have daily devotions with You.

On the other hand, You know that part of the reason I was grouchy was this excruciating pain in my head, neck, shoulders, and back from spending too many hours at the computer, trying to make deadline. Not to mention how grouchy I get when I diet. Thanks for helping me cut back on my food intake yesterday and today. I really feel good about my success. Of course, the real test will be tonight when we order pizza. Help me, Jesus!

Lord, make me the man You want me to be! I don't mind being so different, as long as You're pleased. But enable other people to handle it, too, Jesus—especially Your/my family and church and my readers.

In Your Awesome Name, Holy Jesus!
Amen!

41

Here are some pages you can copy without going to jail

First, a disclaimer: When you write out the Word, I really hope you'll use the *DEVOTION EXPLOSION!* Scripture pages we've provided (see pp. 103–106). It gives you the sense of actually creating a Bible, or a portion thereof, rather than merely writing words on sheets of paper.

Yes, you have my permission to rip these form pages right out of this book and freely copy them for use in your private devotions, or your public devotions, for that matter. That's just the generous kind of guy I am.

And my publisher, Broadman & Holman, is nice folk too. They give you their permission to copy these devotional pages that follow. (Now, don't get carried away and copy anything else out of this book. That would hurt our feelings.)

We make this generous offer because we want to help you encourage your Sunday School classes, your small groups—in fact all your people—to get into God's Word like never before. We say this out of the goodness of our hearts.

We also say this because we're hoping such behavior on your part might make more people want to go out and buy this book.

The Devotion Explosion! Scripture Pages

Book _____ Chapter _____ Verse _____ Date _____

Scripture   Notes

_____   _____

_____   _____

_____   _____

_____   _____

_____   _____

_____   _____

_____   _____

_____   _____

_____   _____

_____   _____

_____   _____

_____   _____

_____   _____

_____   _____

_____   _____

_____   _____

_____   _____

_____   _____

_____   _____

_____   _____

_____   _____

_____   _____

Study: _____   Memorize: _____

☐ Quoted Scripture list ☐ Memorized new Scripture ☐ Wrote in commentary ☐ Prayed

The Devotion Explosion! Scripture Pages

Book _____ Chapter _____ Verse _____ Date _____

Scripture	Notes
_____	_____
_____	_____
_____	_____
_____	_____
_____	_____
_____	_____
_____	_____
_____	_____
_____	_____
_____	_____
_____	_____
_____	_____
_____	_____
_____	_____
_____	_____
_____	_____
_____	_____
_____	_____
_____	_____
_____	_____
_____	_____

Study: _____ Memorize: _____

☐ Quoted Scripture list ☐ Memorized new Scripture ☐ Wrote in commentary ☐ Prayed

The Devotion Explosion! Scripture Pages

Book _____ Chapter _____ Verse _____ Date _____

<table>
<tr><td>Scripture</td><td>Notes</td></tr>
<tr><td>_____</td><td>_____</td></tr>
<tr><td>_____</td><td>_____</td></tr>
<tr><td>_____</td><td>_____</td></tr>
<tr><td>_____</td><td>_____</td></tr>
<tr><td>_____</td><td>_____</td></tr>
<tr><td>_____</td><td>_____</td></tr>
<tr><td>_____</td><td>_____</td></tr>
<tr><td>_____</td><td>_____</td></tr>
<tr><td>_____</td><td>_____</td></tr>
<tr><td>_____</td><td>_____</td></tr>
<tr><td>_____</td><td>_____</td></tr>
<tr><td>_____</td><td>_____</td></tr>
<tr><td>_____</td><td>_____</td></tr>
<tr><td>_____</td><td>_____</td></tr>
<tr><td>_____</td><td>_____</td></tr>
<tr><td>_____</td><td>_____</td></tr>
<tr><td>_____</td><td>_____</td></tr>
<tr><td>_____</td><td>_____</td></tr>
<tr><td>_____</td><td>_____</td></tr>
<tr><td>_____</td><td>_____</td></tr>
<tr><td>_____</td><td>_____</td></tr>
<tr><td>_____</td><td>_____</td></tr>
</table>

Study: _____ Memorize: _____

☐ Quoted Scripture list ☐ Memorized new Scripture ☐ Wrote in commentary ☐ Prayed

The Devotion Explosion! Scripture Pages

Book _____ Chapter _____ Verse _____ Date _____

Scripture	Notes
_____	_____
_____	_____
_____	_____
_____	_____
_____	_____
_____	_____
_____	_____
_____	_____
_____	_____
_____	_____
_____	_____
_____	_____
_____	_____
_____	_____
_____	_____
_____	_____
_____	_____
_____	_____
_____	_____
_____	_____

Study: _____ Memorize: _____

☐ Quoted Scripture list ☐ Memorized new Scripture ☐ Wrote in commentary ☐ Prayed

42

Devotion Explosion! at a glance

These four pages are duplicates of what I've given you elsewhere. But something tells me that for the first month or so, you're going to be turning to them often.

Nice guy that I am, I just thought you might appreciate having this entire book summed up for quick and easy referral, rather than having to flip through the whole book every time.

Your One-of-a-Kind Bible

1. Select a book of the Bible assigned to you by the Holy Spirit.

2. Ask God to open your heart, soul, mind, spirit, and will to the Word you are about to write.

3. Ask the Holy Spirit to speak to you as you write.

4. Read aloud a short phrase, savoring it and absorbing its meaning.

5. Write out the phrase on one of the **DEVOTION EXPLOSION!** pages we have provided (see pp. 103–106).

6. Continue as long as you like, phrase by phrase, verse by verse.

7. Put an asterisk beside any word or phrase that sheds important light on some other Scripture passage you know.

8. Write the book, chapter, and verse of that other passage in the provided margin, creating a cross-reference for better understanding.

9. Record in your **DEVOTION EXPLOSION!** notebook (see chap. 13) anything that makes you go, "Hmmm!" "Huh-oh!" or "Wow!" Include the date, time, and Scripture reference, along with the message you believe God may be giving you.

10. In the slot marked "Study," jot down the reference of any passage you would like to study later.

11. In the slot marked "Memorize," jot down the reference of any passage you would like to hide in your heart through memorization.

12. When you reach a stopping place or you're out of time, thank the Lord for the unspeakable privilege of so intimately handling His Word.

13. Keep your **DEVOTION EXPLOSION!** Scripture pages with you the rest of the day.

14. Pick up tomorrow where you left off today.

High-Tech Prayer Trek

1. Open a password file in your computer and label it "Prayer."

2. Begin your prayer by addressing God as you want to experience Him today.

3. Forget subject quotas, proper wording, and every other stifling restriction—pour out your feelings, requests, confessions, thoughts, fears, obsessions, and desires, in any old order, just as they tumble out of your brain.

4. Observe three rules:

  ▼ Be yourself.

  ▼ Be totally honest.

  ▼ Be alert for what God wants to say back to you.

5. Pray 'til the "ache" goes away or until you run out of time.

6. Delete your prayer.

7. Save the empty file and open it again tomorrow.

Maximum Memorization

1. Select a passage the Holy Spirit assigns you.

2. Write it out on several index cards, saying it aloud as you write it.

3. Place the index cards where you are likely to see them during the day.

4. When in the mood, memorize the passage:

▼ Break up longer passages by memorizing them a verse at a time.

▼ Thoroughly absorb the verse's meaning.

▼ Say the verse aloud, including its reference before and after.

▼ Feel free to quit for the time being as soon as you can say the verse three times in a row without looking.

▼ Look for opportunities throughout the day to quote your new verse during conversations with other people (and in spiritual warfare with Satan).

▼ Come back to the same verse each day until you can say it three times in a row without hesitating and without first having to refer to the card.

▼ Highlight the verse in your Bible.

5. Once memorized, add this verse to the previous verses you have memorized, making a list that you quote once a day.

6. When your list of verses grows so long that it feels too cumbersome to quote daily:

- ▼ ask the Holy Spirit to keep these verses hidden in your heart;
- ▼ ask Him to bring them to mind in the future every time you need them;
- ▼ stop your daily quoting of all the verses on your list—except the ones you just can't live without.

7. Begin a new list by memorizing the next verse—as soon as you get in the mood.

43

What happens when I get ready to move on to something else?

Sooner or later, you're going to quit writing out the Word.

It may be after you finish your one book of the Bible that I challenged you to write as an absolute bare minimum.

It may be after you've written your half-dozen all-time favorites—books like Psalms, Proverbs, Isaiah, John, Acts, Romans.

It may be after you've humbly completed all twenty-seven books of the New Testament. Now they're just a-sittin' up there on your bookshelf, all aglow.

It may be after you run into the same problem I ran into, after twelve years of thrills, chills, and excitement—no more Bible to write.

What then?

Well, you could turn around and start right in on your backup copy, just in case something happens to the first one. Or you may want to write out the Word in another version. I expect that's what I'll do someday. The experience was just too sweet, too awesome, too life-changing, not to repeat.

But what if you want to take a break before starting in on your next book, next testament, or next Bible?

No problem. There are as many legitimate ways to experience God as there are different seasons of your life. Go ahead. Read somebody else's book. Try her system. You'll probably love it. Who knows? I might even provide you with an alternative approach of my own some day, if I can catch some cynical editor on one of her good days and sweet talk her into giving it another go.

But one thing's for sure. If it's legitimate, whatever system you use will take you straight back into your Bible. And here's your secret: Now you have at least one book of the Bible in your own handwriting to explore! The more of the Bible you personally wrote, the more of it you will be able to immerse yourself in as you employ those varying study systems over the seasons of your life. As you will soon discover, the one you penned is a Bible like no other.

Imagine an African coming to America, getting saved, and reading the Bible in his second language, English. Then try to picture what would happen to him, emotionally and spiritually, when a Christian brother gave him for his birthday his very first Wycliffe Bible, translated into Swahili.

That's the impact. That's the difference in having the Bible in your own handwriting: *It's the Word of God in your native language.*

You'll be drawn to it like no other. You'll understand it like no other. You'll love it and accept it and let it change your life like no other. It will usher you into the Holy of Holies of the presence of God like no other.

That's why God commanded His kings to write out their own copy of the Word long, long ago. But that's not all He commanded, remember? *It is to be with him, and he is to read it all the days of his life . . .* (Deut. 17:19).

So do it. Read a piece of your piece of the Word that brings peace. Every day. Even if it's that same favorite passage you read the day before. Even if it's only one verse.

Why? . . . Because if there's one thing someone who has personally written out the very Word of God should know by now, it is this:

If God said to do it, there must be a reason.

44

Alllllllrighty, then! That about sums it up

Thanks for staying with *DEVOTION EXPLOSION!* all the way to the end. If you're anything like me, you've started a lot more books than you've finished.

Come to think of it, you probably are a little bit like me, or you would never have put up with the outrageous style that permeates every page of this book. I confess that although I usually think like this, I don't always write like this. Fear of rejection, I guess.

Do me a favor, would you? Send up a prayer of thanks to the Lord for my editor Janis Whipple and the gang at Broadman & Holman. Down through the years, this huge publishing company has been a pretty traditional outfit. It took enormous courage for them to turn me loose on a project like this and let me fly. They're sure to take some serious heat for it from at least some of their constituency. So just ask God to bless the socks right off of them for breaking the devotional book mold, will you? Thanks.

Hope you enjoyed *DEVOTION EXPLOSION!* As God is my witness, I put my whole heart into it.

One more thing. If you give *DEVOTION EXPLOSION!* a try and it works for you—if it brings you closer to the One who loves you with an everlasting love— tell somebody else about it, will you?

That's all it's going to take to shake this old world—a bunch of us who get so close to Jesus that we just aren't afraid anymore . . . that sin just doesn't look good to us anymore . . . that nobody and nothing can stop us from becoming everything God has called us and enabled us to be.

I'm talking Revival.

If God has used this book to fan your relationship with Him into flame, spread the fire.

▼